FIX IT and
FLIP IT WORKBOOK

FIX IT and FLIP IT WORKBOOK

BY KATIE HAMILTON AND GENE HAMILTON

McGraw Hill

New York   Chicago   San Francisco   Lisbon   London   Madrid
Mexico City   New Delhi   San Juan   Seoul   Singapore   Sydney   Toronto

ISBN: P/N 978-0-07-159773-9 of set
        978-0-07-154416-0
MHID: P/N   0-07-159773-5 of set
        0-07-154416-X

CONTENTS

INTRODUCTION

As newlyweds in 1966, we bought our first fixer-upper, a two-bedroom brick duplex in "needs tender loving care condition." We were teaching school by day and fledging do-it-yourselfers by night, learning new skills (and making many mistakes) as we patched and painted and scraped and tiled. Year after year, house after house, our profits and confidence grew, as we turned to renovating property and writing about it.

We've continued to invest in real estate, and the second edition of *Fix It and Flip It* crystallizes what we've learned. When revising the book, we wanted to include many more of the materials that we developed to analyze property, so we suggested to our publisher that we develop a companion workbook, and here it is.

This workbook contains tools and materials we find useful in the decision process of buying an investment property. No, we're not talking about a toolbox full of hammers and drills; we're referring to analytical tools that help you, the investor, create an objective analysis of potential investment property.

Making money in real estate is not a slam dunk! Purchasing a property, improving it, and selling it for a profit depends on making the right improvements and planning for market forces that, for the most part, are beyond anyone's control. A property that seems like a sure thing in a hot market may not pan out six or eight months later.

Real estate is less liquid than many other investments, and to be successful, it takes a lot of thought and careful analysis to choose the right property to improve and resell, live in, or rent out. The tools in this workbook include checklists, worksheets, estimators, and other lists, all created to help you scrutinize a property so as to understand its potential. By examining a property on paper first, you'll create a more realistic analysis of whether it's worthy of your investment.

We designed this workbook so that you can easily make copies of the materials (and use and reuse them) while analyzing a property and its potential. Use them as your own personal worksheets to get a better understanding of what it takes to invest in real estate by digging into the details of the time and money required.

You'll see that the materials in this workbook follow the format of our book *Fix It and Flip It*, so there's a progression of finding and evaluating a house and crunching the numbers to evaluate its potential, estimate the fix-up costs, and manage the project. In addition, you can download these interactive worksheets and forms from the included CD-Rom. All the worksheets and calculators can be used as is, but many of them are taken from Microsoft Excel spreadsheets that you also can download. You can create your own spreadsheets because most spreadsheet programs function in the same way, so the direction we provide should work for just about any of them.

Like any good workbook, this one has its share of puzzles. In addition, we've included eight *House Word* crossword puzzles. The puzzles are all about houses, using the vocabulary of improving, fixing, buying, and selling houses. We hope that you'll enjoy working them.

When we can, we suggest resources that you'll find on the Internet—interactive forms, calculators, and worksheets—that will help you to analyze a property's potential online.

The workbook begins with the basics in Chapter 1, "Finding the Money." Use the net worth and balance sheets to determine how much money you have and can access. Plug in your numbers to the loan calculator, and learn how much money you can borrow. Compile the material, keep it updated, and use it as a basis for your real estate investment notebook. It will be useful at tax time, too.

In Chapter 2, "Evaluating Property," you'll see that there are profiles for a single residence and a condominium. Make several copies of the "Property Profile" when you look at houses of interest to document what you see. You'll find two types of profiles—comprehensive and extremely detailed and at-a-glance for those quick walk-throughs with a camera or recorder. Make notes in the "Image/Recorder Reference" to be certain that you don't miss any key components of the house. Some might say that our approach verges on the obsessive, but we know from experience that *you can't have too much information about a house if you're considering its purchase.*

In Chapter 3, "Doing the Math," the dollars and cents become real because you're getting serious about committing to an investment. You may find that you've narrowed your selection down to more than one investment property and are faced with several possibilities. Should you fix it up and sell, expand its space, live in it, fix it and then sell it later, or fix it up and rent it out? Use the comparable house evaluation sheets to make an analysis and decide which offers the best potential as an investment.

Chapter 4, "Buying and Selling Property," is about the critical moment. At this time, the deal is being finalized, home inspectors have been called, and you're getting ready to close. The checklists and worksheets in this section will help you to expedite the transaction and realize your investment goal and make you confident that you've covered all the bases.

You'll find cost estimators for a full range of improvement projects in Chapter 5, "Estimating Fix-Up Costs," which you'll probably refer to often. The project calculators cover a wide range of jobs—painting a room, installing flooring, laying sod—just to name a few. You'll find these tools invaluable and become familiar with using them to cost out your planned improvements.

In Chapter 6, "Space-Expanding Possibilities," you'll find information about more extensive improvements to a house. For a major project such as remodeling a kitchen or bathroom or converting an attic, basement, or porch to usable living space, you'll find worksheets to guide you through the job. Make copies and use them to analyze the potential of expansion.

The worksheets in Chapter 7, "Managing the Job," are tools to help you to direct a rehab project. Use the checklist to keep the project on track and the cost worksheet to control the dollars. When you're a part-time investor managing a rehab, these materials will keep you on the straight and narrow path to realizing your goal.

Many investors find rehabbing to rent a successful strategy. In Chapter 8, "Renting as a Fallback Strategy," you'll find a loan calculator and checklist for finding a good tenant and a worksheet to manage rental property.

We wish you success in your real estate investments and hope that this workbook helps you to plan, analyze, and realize their potential. You can reach us at our Web site www.diyornot.com.

CHAPTER 1

FINDING THE MONEY

The era when banks were literally throwing money at people is over. The credit markets have come back to reality, and the banks are looking to lend money to qualified individuals with decent credit.

As with any business, buying property, improving it, and then selling or renting it requires working capital. How much capital depends on your creativity and resourcefulness, as well as on the scope of your projects. One of the first steps to take is to decide how much you can afford to invest because no investing is totally risk-free, and this is true for investing in real estate as well.

It's difficult to decide what you can set aside to invest if you don't have a good handle on what you have. Also, the first question the loan officer will ask is for you to produce a balance sheet showing what you own and what you owe. If you already use personal financial software such as Quicken or Microsoft Money, all you have to do is run the "Net Worth" report. If you don't have the software, use the worksheets in this chapter to put your financial ducks in order.

There are several ways of looking at net worth, so we provide a worksheet you can use to find your personal net worth and a slightly different form that a business would use.

Whenever we are evaluating a property, an important question we ask is: How much will the financing cost? There are many mortgage calculators on the Internet, but we have included a simple-to-use tool that saves a lot of time.

Personal Balance Sheet

This is basic accounting. Take a look at the "Personal Balance Sheet (Net Worth)" form that follows, and you'll see that there are two sections. The top of the form itemizes the value of your assets, such as savings accounts, insurance, cars, the market value of your house, investments, and retirement accounts such as IRAs and 401(k)s. The lower section lists all your debts, including mortgages, credit-card debt, car loans, personal loans, and outstanding bills.

When you subtract the dollar total in the lower section from the upper section, you have a good idea of your net worth. You may be surprised at the figure, pleasantly surprised or disappointed; either way, it gives you a realistic picture of your financial condition at this point in time.

Most lending institutions are interested in the total of what you own and also what you owe to creditors on a yearly basis. These are called *current assets* and *liabilities*, and they give lenders a good idea of how much money you have to pay this year on your debts as compared with your annual earnings. Assets and debt that stretch over a longer period are consider long term and represent assets and debt that may be paid in a future period.

When you are gathering up your checking and savings account information, copy down the names of the banks and account numbers where you do business. The lending institution will want this information, but don't put it on your balance sheet because you may want to give this document to people who don't require such information.

The current assets section should include your checking and savings accounts and the portion of any notes or other assets that you will receive in the current year. Let's say that you lent $5,000 to someone over a five-year period, and you expect to get $1,000 repaid this year. The $1,000 is placed in the current assets area and the $4,000 in the long-term assets area.

The same goes for the liabilities. Put the portion of your mortgage you pay this year and the part of any loans that are due this year in the current liabilities area. The outstanding balances at the end of the year go in the long-term liabilities area.

Of course, the total assets minus the total liabilities equals your net worth. What the figure shows is how much capital you actually own. For example, you may have thousands of dollars worth of cars, a boat, and a big house worth a million dollars, but you may owe the bank 95 percent of what these assets are worth. In this case, your net worth is less than $50,000. Not bad, but nowhere near appearances. This is why the lender is interested in your personal balance sheet and not the brand of car you drive.

PERSONAL BALANCE SHEET (NET WORTH)

Date

Assets

  Current Assets

    Cash—checking accounts   _____

    Cash—savings accounts   _____

    Current portion of notes owed to you   _____

    Other current assets   _____

  Total Current Assets $ _____

  Long-Term Assets

    Long-term portion of notes   _____

    Certificates of deposit   _____

    Life insurance (cash value)   _____

    Securities (stocks, bonds, etc.)   _____

    Real estate (market value)   _____

    Vehicles (market value)   _____

    Individual retirement plans, etc.   _____

    Other long-term assets   _____

  Total Long-Term Assets $ _____

Total Assets $ _____

Liabilities

  Current Liabilities

    Current bills—you owe   _____

    Current portion of mortgages on real estate   _____

    Current portion of loans   _____

    Current portion of taxes   _____

  Total Current Liabilities $ _____

  Long-Term Liabilities

    Mortgages on real estate   _____

    Notes cosigned, etc.   _____

    Loans—you owe   _____

    Taxes—you owe   _____

    Other liabilities   _____

  Total Long-Term Liabilities $ _____

Total Liabilities $ _____

Net Worth (total assets – total liabilities) $ _____

Business-Type Balance Sheet

The balance sheet for a business uses the same information but arranges it in a different way. The most common method of tracking the activity of a business is with a double-entry accounting system. This system takes a company's assets and matches them against its liabilities and owner's equity. The owners equity section is similar to an individual's net worth in that it represents the value of the owner's portion of the company.

The books are said to be *in balance* when the assets equal the liabilities plus the owner's equity. As your investing grows, it's a good idea to start separating your investing activity from your personal business.

On the type of form that follows, you would list assets such as cash in your business account, the cost of the equipment and tools you purchased for renovation work, the cost of the property you purchased as an investment, and any monies owed to you in connection with your investment activities.

The titles of the items in the liabilities section are straightforward—basically, what you owe to the bank, venders, and credit-card companies. The owner's equity is the difference between the assets and liabilities. At the start of the business, owner's equity is zero.

If you sell the house and make a profit, you deposit the money in the bank, which is shown in the cash account. This account will go up more than the value of the property you remove from the property asset account. Of course, the liability accounts also would go down because you pay off the mortgage and other loans. Thus the asset accounts minus the liability accounts equal the profit, and unless you spend it right away on purchasing other property, it is reflected in the retained earnings account to balance the books.

The "Business-Type Balance Sheet" that follows is a snapshot of your business at a particular time. When you purchase new property, the cash goes down as the property assets go up. The liability account also goes up to reflect the mortgage and other loans associated with the purchase, so the sheet stays in balance.

You may not always make a profit, and the liabilities may be larger than the assets, in which case the retained earnings are a negative number (or a loss), but when they are added to (actually subtracted from) the liabilities, the result is still the net assets.

So much for "Accounting 101," eventually, you will need to look at your real estate investments as a business, and this simple form is designed to get you going.

BUSINESS-TYPE BALANCE SHEET

As of:

Current Assets

Cash _____

Tools _____

Purchased materials _____

Total Current Assets $ _____

Property at cost _____

Notes receivable _____

Intangibles _____

Other Assets $ _____

Total Assets $ _____

Current Liabilities

Construction loans _____

Payments to contractors _____

Charge accounts _____

Taxes payable _____

Total Current Liabilities $ _____

Long-term debt (mortgage) _____

Total Long-Term Liabilities $ _____

Total Liabilities $ _____

Owners Equity

Retained earnings _____

Total Net Worth $ _____

Total Liabilities & Net Worth $ _____

Instructions for Loan Calculator

Following is a simple "Loan Calculator." You enter three variables: the amount you want to borrow, the interest rate, and the length of time of the loan. The calculator will figure out what your monthly payment will be.

Of course, in order for the calculator to work, you must have a spreadsheet type of program. Microsoft Excel is one popular spreadsheet program, and its file format can be read by most other types.

All the spreadsheet programs work in the same way. The rows and columns are labeled, and the interactions of these rows and columns form cells. Formulas then are assigned to the cells, and the spreadsheet does the calculations for you.

The top figure is a sample of what the calculator looks like in Excel. The lower figure shows the labeling of the rows and columns of the spreadsheet. All you have to do is type the formula into cell D8. The spreadsheet will take the value of the loan amount from cell D5, the interest rate from cell D6, the loan term from cell D7, and enter them into the formula and calculate the payment.

The financial formula used to calculate a loan payment is built into Excel and most other spreadsheet programs as the PMT function. This function is simpler to use than entering the actual formula for calculating the payment. Type into cell D8 this function: =PMT(D6/12,D7*12,D5,0,0). If your spreadsheet program does not have a PMT function, then type in this formula instead: =(D6/12)/(1-((1+(D6/12))^(-D7)))*D5.

Loan Calculator

Loan amount:
Annual interest rate:
Term in years:
Monthly payment: $

	A	B	C	D	E
1					
2					
3		**Loan Calculator**			
4					
5		Loan amount:			
6		Annual interest rate:			
7		Term in years:			
8		Monthly payment:		$	
9					

Test your calculator for accuracy by comparing the payment it calculates at different loan amounts, interest rates, and terms with the payments calculated by the calculator at BankRate.com (http://bankrate.com/brm/popcalc2.asp).

 You can download these interactive worksheets and forms from the included CD-Rom.

Here are some other Web sites where you'll find interactive personal finance forms to download: Bankrate.com, LendingTree.com, and MSNBC.com.

EVALUATING PROPERTY

For each property you're considering, fill out a property profile to record your first impression and all the details that you observe. You're ready to start evaluating property after you've chosen the areas and neighborhoods that you feel have potential. Running down leads, going to open houses, and making appointments to see a house takes considerable time. It's a lot like prospecting, and it's a good idea to document what you see rather than relying on your memory.

In this chapter you'll see there are property profiles for single-residence homes and condominiums in two forms. The short versions are at-a-glance profiles, and the more detailed are comprehensive profiles. Use these profiles to gather information on each property in an organized and orderly way.

Of course, you should be looking at as many properties as possible and keeping the basic information available for comparison. This is where the property comparison worksheet will be a big help. There is a comparison worksheet for single residences and condos. By looking at the specific details of each property in a side-by-side comparison, you can get a better picture of the relative strengths and weaknesses of each property.

 You can download the digital versions of these worksheets from the included CD-Rom.

Property Profile Instructions

Whether you're a natural-born list maker or not, it's important to develop this skill when you are evaluating property. When you are analyzing a potential investment, you can't have too much information, and when it's documented in a coherent form, all the better.

We've designed two forms of the property profile, one for a quick look and the other for a more comprehensive appraisal. They both detail the many fine points you'll want to consider. The "Comprehensive Property Profile" is more than double the length of the "At-a-Glance Property Profile," so choose the profile best suited to you and the property you're evaluating.

You undoubtedly will have a listing sheet on the property, but that's not nearly enough to base a "buy" decision on. Use the profile to confirm the overview information on the listing sheet, but take your own room measurements and evaluate everything you see.

Download the digital versions or copy or scan these comprehensive and at-a-glance property profile sheets and customize them to the types of houses in your area. For example, if the houses have no basements, delete that category. This will make them more efficient for your use.

Spend some time reviewing the items on the profile sheets before you arrive at a property so that you can make the checklist work for you and your style of observation. For each property, record the address and date you visited. In the "Notes" area, you may find that a cryptic "OK" is all that's needed. Or you may want to detail items of interest or concern. Use the area to jot down anything that strikes you as particularly notable or questionable.

Use the right-hand column, "Image Recorder Reference," to keep track of any pictures or video you take with your digital camera or cell phone. Since most digital cameras name the image as it is taken, you can jot down the photo ID as you walk through the property. Later, download the pictures to your computer, and place them in a folder for easy reference. If you download the MS Word document or make your own, you can import the picture into the form and create a comprehensive document containing both your notes and the visuals.

A digital voice recorder and voice-to-text software can be used to evaluate property, and the text can be edited on the computer and placed with the pictures into the profile for easy review later. If they are too long to fit into the "Notes" section, block them and make a reference to them in the right-hand column.

Theses profile sheets can become the central depository for all the information you collect. You may want to expand the profiles to contain information that you get from the real estate agent and other sources, especially on the potential for improving the property.

		Page 1
COMPREHENSIVE PROPERTY PROFILE		

Address:
Date of inspection:
Agent:

INSPECTION ITEMS	NOTES	Image Recorder Reference
Exterior Entrances		
Walkways, driveway, and stairs		
Lawn, plantings, and trees		
Doors and location		
Living, Dining, Family Rooms		
Walls and ceilings		
Doors and windows		
Flooring		
Lighting fixtures		
Number of electric outlets		
Built-ins or fireplace		
Closets		
Other features		

		Page 2
COMPREHENSIVE PROPERTY PROFILE		
INSPECTION ITEMS	NOTES	Image Recorder Reference
Bathroom 1		
Walls and ceiling		
Doors and windows		
Flooring		
Lighting fixtures		
Number of GFCI electric outlets		
Cabinets		
Countertops		
Ventilation		
Tub/shower		
Toilet		
Sink and faucet		
Closets		
Other features		
Bathroom 2		
Walls and ceiling		
Doors and windows		
Flooring		

		Page 3
COMPREHENSIVE PROPERTY PROFILE		
INSPECTION ITEMS	NOTES	Image Recorder Reference
Lighting fixtures		
Number of GFCI electric outlets		
Cabinets		
Countertops		
Ventilation		
Tub/shower		
Toilet		
Sink and faucet		
Closets		
Other features		
Kitchen		
Walls and ceilings		
Doors and windows		
Flooring		
Lighting fixtures		
Number of GFCI electric outlets		
Cabinets/islands		
Countertops		
Ventilation		

		Page 4
COMPREHENSIVE PROPERTY PROFILE		
INSPECTION ITEMS	NOTES	Image Recorder Reference
Appliances and their power sources		
Range Refrigerator Dishwasher Disposal		
Sink and faucet		
Other features		
Bedroom 1		
Walls and ceilings		
Doors and windows		
Flooring		
Lighting fixtures		
Number of electric outlets		
Built-ins or fireplace		
Closets		
Other features		
Bedroom 2		
Walls and ceilings		
Doors and windows		
Flooring		
Lighting fixtures		

		Page 5
COMPREHENSIVE PROPERTY PROFILE		
INSPECTION ITEMS	NOTES	Image Recorder Reference
Number of electric outlets		
Built-ins or fireplace		
Closets		
Other features		
Bedroom 3		
Walls and ceilings		
Doors and windows		
Flooring		
Lighting fixtures		
Number of electric outlets		
Built-ins or fireplace		
Closets		
Other features		
Additional room		
Walls and ceilings		
Doors and windows		
Flooring		
Lighting fixtures		

		Page 6
COMPREHENSIVE PROPERTY PROFILE		
INSPECTION ITEMS	NOTES	Image Recorder Reference
Number of electric outlets		
Built-ins or fireplace		
Closets		
Other features		
Attic		
Walls and framing		
Signs of water damage		
Unfinished (usable as storage)		
Thickness of insulation		
Max. ceiling height		
Location of stairs		
Electrical and lighting		
Finished (living space)		
Walls and ceilings		
Doors and windows		
Flooring		
Number of electric outlets		

		Page 7
COMPREHENSIVE PROPERTY PROFILE		
INSPECTION ITEMS	NOTES	Image Recorder Reference
Lighting fixtures		
Closet or storage		
Other features		
Basement		
Walls and framing signs of termite or pest damage		
Unfinished (usable as storage)		
High water mark sign on walls or floor		
Height of lowest pipe or duct		
Location of stairs		
Location of exterior access		
Proximity to furnace		
Finished (living space)		
Walls and ceilings		
Doors and windows		
Flooring		
Number of electric outlets		

COMPREHENSIVE PROPERTY PROFILE

INSPECTION ITEMS	NOTES	Image Recorder Reference
Lighting fixtures		
Closet or storage		
Sump pump		
Ventilation		
Other features		
Laundry or Utility Closet		
Wash tub		
Number of GFCI electric outlets		
Power source for washer/dryer		
Washer/dryer units		
Other features		
Systems and Mechanics		
Electrical panel location		
Amperage and voltage rating		
Number of circuits, limited or expandable		
Heating system		

		Page 9
COMPREHENSIVE PROPERTY PROFILE		
INSPECTION ITEMS	NOTES	Image Recorder Reference
Air conditioning system or window units		
Hot water heater		
Water-softening system		
Exterior of house		
Doors and windows		
Storm doors and windows		
Siding		
Roof tight, missing or curling shingles		
Chimney, loose bricks or flashing		
Porches		
Screens, potential to enclose		
Decks		
Boards and fastener Stairs and railing		
Patio		
Drainage and gutters and downspouts		

		Page 10
COMPREHENSIVE PROPERTY PROFILE		
INSPECTION ITEMS	NOTES	Image Recorder Reference
Pooling water around foundation		
Foundation and crawl space		
Signs of termite or pest damage		
Wet or dry		
Insulation		
Ventilation		
Garage and Outbuildings		
Foundation and soundness of structure		
Condition of siding, doors		
Windows		
Signs of termite or pest damage		
Lawn and Garden		
Fencing, location of posts		
Who owns the fence?		
Does it mark property line?		

		Page 11
COMPREHENSIVE PROPERTY PROFILE		
INSPECTION ITEMS	NOTES	Image Recorder Reference
Lawn and landscaping grass		
Walkways		
Shrubbery and plantings		
Trees		
Yard structures or obstacles		

AT-A-GLANCE PROPERTY PROFILE		Page 1

Address:
Date of Viewing:

INSPECTION ITEMS	NOTES	Image Recorder Reference
Drive-Up First Impression		
Overall condition		
Curb appeal		
Sidewalks		
Front entry		
Living and Dining Rooms		
Overall condition		
Flooring		
Lighting		
Fireplace, built-ins		
Windows		
Other features		
Family Room		
Overall condition		
Flooring		
Lighting		
Fireplace, built-ins		
Windows		
Other features		
Kitchen		
Overall condition		
Cabinets and countertops		
Sinks and faucets		
Appliances		
Flooring		
Lighting		
No. of GFCI electric outlets		

		Page 2
AT-A-GLANCE PROPERTY PROFILE		
INSPECTION ITEMS	NOTES	Image Recorder Reference
Bathroom 1		
Overall condition		
Vanity and countertop		
Medicine cabinet		
Storage		
Plumbing fixtures		
Flooring		
Lighting		
Ventilation		
No. of GFCI electric outlets		
Windows		
Access panel to tub/shower		
Other features		
Bathroom 2		
Overall condition		
Vanity and countertop		
Medicine cabinet		
Storage		
Plumbing fixtures		
Flooring		
Lighting		
Ventilation		
No. of GFCI electric outlets		
Windows		
Access panel to tub/shower		
Other features		

AT-A-GLANCE PROPERTY PROFILE

INSPECTION ITEMS	NOTES	Image Recorder Reference
Bedroom 1		
Overall condition		
Flooring		
Windows		
No. of electric outlets		
Lighting		
Closets		
Other features		
Bedroom 2		
Overall condition		
Flooring		
Windows		
No. of electric outlets		
Lighting		
Closets		
Other features		
Bedroom 3		
Overall condition		
Flooring		
Windows		
No. of electric outlets		
Lighting		
Closets		
Other features		
Attic		
Stairs or access		
Finished—overall condition		
Unfinished—usable as storage or convertible to living space		

		Page 4
AT-A-GLANCE PROPERTY PROFILE		
INSPECTION ITEMS	NOTES	Image Recorder Reference
Roof Ventilation Signs of pest or animal damage		
Basement Stairs or access-egress Finished—overall condition Unfinished—usable as storage or convertible to living space Floor joists Signs of pest or animal damage Signs of water damage Sump pump		
Laundry Washer–dryer appliances Power source Washtub		
Systems and Mechanics Electrical panel—amperage and voltage rating; no. of circuits; limited or expandable; no. of electric outlets		

AT-A-GLANCE PROPERTY PROFILE

INSPECTION ITEMS	NOTES	Image Recorder Reference
Heating/Cooling System		
Hot water heater		
Water softening system		
Sewer		
Exterior of House—Walk Around		
Overall condition		
Facade: Siding, masonry		
Doors and windows		
Roof and chimney		
Decks, porches		
Drainage and gutters		
Foundation and crawl space		
Driveway		
Garage		
Outbuildings		
Land grading, drainage		
Retaining wall		
Yard proximity to neighbors		
Landscaping		
Overall condition		
Lawn		
Trees, shrubbery		
Garden beds		
Fencing		
Walkways		

Comparison Worksheet Instructions

We've all heard the importance of comparing apples with apples and not apples with oranges, and the same is true for comparing investment properties. After you have used the profiles to compile data on properties in which you are considering investing, you need an efficient method to compare them, so we developed the following simple comparison worksheets.

Use the "Single-Residence Comparison Worksheet" to compare property in a specific price range, neighborhood, or whatever criterion you determined will influence its value the most. Using the worksheets gives you a snapshot view of each property and can help you to distill the fine points to consider. You may have narrowed your search to property within a specific school district, for example, and can use a comparison of the features of houses within that area.

The "Condo Comparison Worksheet" goes a long way to help you decide between similar units, which may or may not have the same improved features that enhance their value. When there are three two-bedroom, two-bath condo units all in the same complex, it takes some careful evaluation. For example, all three units may be in good condition, but if one has a stunning view of a bubbling brook, it probably will be more desirable than one overlooking a parking lot. Use the "Positives" and "Negatives" section to note these features to help you make a decision.

For more general observations that you feel will influence the value of a unit, use "Other considerations." Also, at the bottom of both these worksheets is a row labeled "Comp. property selling price." If you can find comparable property that has sold recently, enter that information here.

After you have used the other worksheets we provide to evaluate your prospective property, you also may want to modify this sheet to include customized rows where you can compare your planned improvements and the extra value you estimate they will add to the property.

SINGLE-RESIDENCE COMPARISON WORKSHEET				
	Property 1	Property 2	Property 3	Property 4
Address				
Listing date				
Asking price				
No. of bedrooms				
No. of bathrooms				
Approx. sq. ft.				
Lot sq. ft.				
Basement				
Garage				
Deck or patio				
Porch				
Taxes				
Year built				
School district				
Positives				
Negatives				
Other considerations				
Comp. property selling price				
Date				

CONDO COMPARISON WORKSHEET				
	Property 1	Property 2	Property 3	Property 4
Address				
Listing date				
Asking price				
No. of bedrooms				
No. of bathrooms				
Approx. sq. ft.				
Cost per sq. ft				
Parking space				
Garage				
Storage space				
Deck or patio				
Taxes				
Year built				
Monthly fee				
Assoc. fee				
School district				
Positives				
Negatives				
Complex amenities				
Rental restrictions				
Other considerations				
Comp. property selling price				
Date				

CHAPTER 3

DOING THE MATH

The worksheets in this chapter deal with the dollars and cents of investing in a house to resell. However you look at it, the profit has to come from the difference between the purchase price and the sale price—and that difference must be large enough to cover all the costs.

Our formula is simple: The sales price minus the purchase price and costs equals the profit. You make your money when you buy the house, assuming that you don't pay too much for it. Look at the three variables in this equation and see that each is made up of many smaller variables. Some of these variables you can control, such as the purchase price and fix-up costs, whereas others, such as the selling price, you can estimate, but ultimately, the market will set its value.

Property Analysis Worksheet

The "Property Analysis Worksheet" in this section allows you to calculate the purchase price that you can afford to pay and expect to make a profit. The worksheet is designed to allow you to create a lot of "what if" scenarios. Many of the variables on these forms will have to be educated estimates, and we will give you some help there, but the most important function of the worksheet is to help you develop a plan and then put the numbers on paper in an organized fashion.

The top of the worksheet helps you to calculate the "Target Purchase Price." Here is a rundown of what the different variables on the worksheet are for:

The "Estimated Improved Value" figure is just that—an estimate. We suggest that you use real estate Web sites to look at comparable property. This would be property comparable with the fixed-up property you are considering. The search results will give you a ballpark idea of the value of the house, or at least current asking prices. Your real estate broker also can prepare a market analysis of comparable houses that have sold recently. This list will give you actual selling prices of similar properties.

The next variables in the profit equation are the costs of purchasing and holding the property, costs of all planned repairs and improvements, sales costs, and, of course, profit. Some of the costs are easier to calculate. Here is a rundown of the major costs involved in fixing up a property for resale:

At the closing of a real estate deal, certain costs of the transaction are apportioned to the buyer and to the seller. The buyer pays for an appraisal, survey, property transfer taxes, and legal fees. If the real estate taxes are paid, then a rebate is given the seller; if not, the seller pays for his or her share of the tax bill. Of course, you also have to settle up with the bank and pay any fees the bank requires to execute the loan. Most of the fees and taxes are set fees or a percentage of the sales price. It is possible to make an accurate estimate of what these costs will be. (See Chapter 4 for a copy of a typical Settlement Statement.)

The "Holding Costs" include interest on the loan, property taxes, insurance and utilities. The length of time you plan to hold the property affects these costs. Unless the project can be turned around in a month or so and put back on the market, use a year as the standard holding time.

While it's essential that you have a good idea what repair and improvement costs will be, you're working against the clock to pull them together. If the property has potential, other investors will be interested and may be able to act more quickly than you can. (Chapter 5 provides calculators to figure repair costs to help you compile an estimate for the cost of several typical improvement projects.)

The repairs and improvements costs represent a major portion of the project's overall expense. If, after you calculate the total cost, you arrive at an unrealistically low purchase price, some adjustments are in order. In some cases the market will not support a selling price high enough to cover the costs of the repairs and improvements and return a decent profit; if this is the case, it's better to find out before you purchase the property. As with any other business, fixing up property for resale has its risks. This is what the contingency fund is all about.

Every real estate transaction has costs to both the seller and the purchaser. We estimate these costs separately from the sales costs because the value of the property is different.

The profit line is considered an expense because the difference between the purchase price and selling price must contain the profit. The figure is the actual cash that you hope to realize after the dust settles, the property is sold, and all loans and bills are paid.

The most important line in this worksheet is the purchase price. Much of your potential profit is determined the moment you settle on a price. If you overpay for the property, the added value of your improvements can't be fully realized.

You must purchase the property at a low enough price to afford the necessary improvements for the property to reach its full market value. With this in mind, you must establish a purchase price that we call the "Target Purchase Price" for the property that ensures that you don't overpay.

The target purchase price that you can afford to pay for a particular property may be far from what the seller has in mind. Remember that the true value of any property is what a buyer will pay, *not* what the seller is asking. Of course, this is important to remember because we eventually will swap places and become the seller.

The lower section of the worksheet allows you to analyze the sale of the property. Here, you estimate the sale price after all repairs and improvements are completed. Then the sales costs are taken into account, and a gross profit is calculated. After the holding and sale costs are accounted for, the net profit and a return on investment is calculated.

Here again, come selling time, you will have hard figures for your costs. For example, if an offer comes in a bit lower than expected, with this sheet as reference, you can quickly see the affect a lower selling price will have on your profit.

In *Fix It and Flip It*, we give an example of how this worksheet can be used. Following is a copy of a completed worksheet for the purchase of a single story two-bedroom, one-and-a-half-bath home in poor condition. Let's say that after completing a market analysis of comparable property we decided that the house would be worth at least $250,000 with repairs and improvements completed. We'd enter that figure in the "Estimated Improved Value" row and then subtract estimated costs for closing, holding, and repairs estimated at $26,500.

We anticipated and subtracted a $2,000 contingency fund and an $8,000 profit, as well as estimated sales costs of $15,000. The result would be our target purchase price of $198,500. Changing any of the preceding figures, of

	A	B	C	D	E	F	G	H
1								
2								
3		**Property Analysis Worksheet**						
4								
5								
6		Estimated Improved Value						
7		Closing Costs						
8		Holding Costs						
9		Repairs						
10		Total Expenses				$	-	
11		Contingency						
12		Profit						
13		Total Contingency/Profit				$	-	
14		Estimated Sales Costs						
15		Target Purchase Price				$	-	
16								
17		10 Percent Down		$	-			
18		First Mortgage		$	-			
19		Construction Loan		$	-			
20								
21		**Sale**						
22		Sale Price						
23		Cost				$	-	
24		Gross Profit				$	-	
25		Real Estate Commission						
26		Overbudget Expenses						
27		Holding/construction		$	-			
28		Total Costs				$	-	
29		Net				$	-	
30		Investment				$	-	
31		Return on Investment (before Taxes)			0%			
32								
33		**Cash Flow**						
34		Sale				$	-	
35		Repay First Mortgage		$	-			
36		Repay Construction Loan		$	-			
37		Closing Costs		$	-			
38		Cash out				$	-	
39		Investment				$	-	
40		Profit				$	-	
41		Return on Investment (before Taxes)			0%			
42								

course, goes right to the bottom line of the target purchase price, which is what we would try to purchase the property for. If we could not come to some agreement with the seller, we'd reconsider the extent of the renovation and rework the numbers. But if they don't work out, we would look for another property.

After putting 10 percent down, the standard mortgage would be in the amount of $178,650. Since we planned on using the bank's money, we have a construction loan of $26,500.

The sale of the property works in the same way. All costs are taken from the selling price to arrive at a net profit. This is an essential worksheet when you are in negotiation with a buyer. All the cost figures except the real estate commission are known, so a change in sales price goes directly to the net profit.

The worksheet is quicker and easier to use if you make it into a spreadsheet. The arithmetic is done automatically whenever you change one of the variables. You can download the spreadsheet or make your own.

All the variables and calculated fields in the spreadsheet are in columns E and H. Here is a quick rundown of the cell content: After constructing the spreadsheet, test it by entering the same numbers used in the sample spreadsheet; your spreadsheet should produce the same results.

G10=SUM(E7:E9)

G13=SUM(E11:E12)

G15=G6-SUM(G7:G14)

G23=G15

G24=G22-G23

G28=SUM(E25:E27)

G29=G24-G28

G30=E17

G34=G22

G38=G34-SUM(E35:E37)

G39=E17

G40=G38-G39

E27=G10

E31=IF(OR(G30=0,G29=0),0,G29/G30)

E35=E18

PROPERTY ANALYSIS WORKSHEET

Estimated Improved Value		$250,000.00
Closing Costs	$1,500.00	
Holding Costs	$10,000.00	
Repairs	$15,000.00	
Total Expenses		$26,500.00
Contingency	$26,500.00	
Profit	$8,000.00	
Total Contingency/Profit		$10,000.00
Estimated Sales Costs		$15,000.00
Target Purchase Price		$198,500.00
10 Percent Down	$19,850.00	
First Mortgage	$178,650.00	
Construction Loan	$26,500.00	

Sale

Sale Price		$246,000.00
Cost		$198,500.00
Gross Profit		$47,500.00
Real Estate Commission	$14,760.00	
Overbudget Expenses	$1,000.00	
Holding/construction	$26,500.00	
Total Costs		$42,260.00
Net		$5,240.00
Investment		$19,850.00
Return on Investment (before Taxes)	26%	

Cash Flow

Sale		$246,000.00
Repay First Mortgage	$178,650.00	
Repay Construction Loan	$26,500.00	
Closing Costs	$15,760.00	
Cash Out		$25,090.00
Investment		$19,850.00
Profit		$5,240.00
Return on Investment (before Taxes)	26%	

E36=E19

E37=E25+E26

E41=IF(OR(G39=0,G40=0),0,G29/G40)

Live-in Property Analysis Worksheet

Time is a key variable because owning real estate has costs—interest on the loan, taxes, utilities, and items like that. The longer you own the property, the more costs you incur. However, over that same period, most real estate appreciates in value, and this historically has offset the costs. Unless the local real estate market is hot, appreciation rates over a short time usually won't cover the holding costs. Open that horizon to several years or more, however, and the property can appreciate enough to cover these costs. This is one of the most appealing characteristics of a real estate investment.

This worksheet analyzes the potential profit of a property that you may hold for several years. You can use this worksheet to analyze a property that you plan to live in while you make improvements. It is only practical as a spreadsheet because there are several financial formulas that you really can't do by hand.

The top of the spreadsheet contains the variables, and the lower portion contains the analysis. For example, in the completed spreadsheet, after you enter the cost and other data, such as the rate of the loan and the amount you want to put down, the spreadsheet calculates the mortgage payment and other expenses such as the real estate commission, expected yearly appreciation, and holding period.

In the example that follows, the property is small, inexpensive, and in poor condition. The plan calls for a complete renovation costing $20,000 with an estimated improved value of $215,000. The project has conventional financing for both the purchase and a construction loan at 7 percent. The plan also has provisions for the sale by a real estate agent. The yearly appreciation is hoped to be at least 3 percent. The two sections of the spreadsheet compare the potential profit if the house were sold in a year or held for three years.

Use this spreadsheet to run several scenarios because it is easy to change the variables at the top of the sheet. Set the sales commission to zero and see how that affects the bottom line.

Time is money. As you can see, the holding cost easily overcomes any appreciation of the house. It will take over 8 percent annual appreciation to cover the holding costs. Now, if you were living in the house, then the overhead is really the cost of living, like paying rent, so the situation may not be so bad. You also probably would want to pay down the construction loan, but that may not be possible until you get the cash from the house sale.

LIVE-IN PROPERTY ANALYSIS WORKSHEET

Cost		Sales Agent Rate %	
Improvements		Yearly Appreciation %	
Downpayment %		Holding Period (years)	
Downpayment amount	$ -	Est. Improved Sale Price	
Loan	$ -		
Mgt. Rate			
Mgt. Time			
Insurance, Taxes			
Condo Fee			
Misc. Maintenance			

	---------- One Year -------------	---------- Over Time ------------
Expense		
Mgt. Payment	$ -	$ -
Construction Loan Pmt.	$ -	$ -
Insurance, Taxes	$ -	$ -
Misc. Maintenance	$ -	$ -
Condo Fees	$ -	$ -
Total Exp.	$ -	$ -
Anticipated Sale		
Cost/Improved Value	$ -	$ -
Increase	$ -	$ -
Future Value	$ -	$ -
Pay Mgt.	$ -	$ -
Pay Construction Loan	$ -	$ -
Cash repayments	$ -	$ -
Gross Cash from Sale	$ -	$ -
Sales Cost	$ -	$ -
Operating Cost	$ -	$ -
Total Costs	$ -	$ -
Gross Cash	$ -	$ -
Investment (Downpayment)	$ -	$ -
Operating Cost	$ -	$ -
Total Out of Pocket	$ -	$ -
Net Profit	$ -	$ -
Return on Investment	0%	0%

Live-in Property Analysis Worksheet

Cost	$150,000.00		Sales Agent Rate %		5%
Improvements	$20,000.00		Yearly Appreciation %		3%
Downpayment	10%		Holdng Period (years)		3
Downpayment amount	$15,000.00		Est. Improved Sale Price	$215,000.00	
Loan	$135,000.00				
Mgt. Rate	7.0%				
Mgt. Time	30				
Insurance, Taxes	$1,500.00				
Condo Fee					
Misc. Maintenance	$250.00				

---------- One Year ---------------------- Over Time ------------

Expense

	One Year	Over Time
Mgt. Payment	$10,879.16	$32,637.49
Construction Loan Pmt.	$1,611.73	$4,835.18
Insurance, Taxes	$1,500.00	$4,500.00
Misc. Maintenance	$250.00	$750.00
Condo Fees	$	$
Total Exp.	$14,240.89	$42,722.68

Anticipated Sale

	One Year	Over Time
Cost/Improved Value	$215,000.00	$215,000.00
Increase	$4,500.00	$19,936.31
Future Value	$219,500.00	$234,936.31
Pay Mgt.	$135,000.00	$135,000.00
Pay Construction Loan	$20,000.00	$20,000.00
Cash repayments	$155,000.00	$155,000.00
Gross Cash from Sale	$64,500.00	$79,936.31
Sales Cost	$10,975.00	$11,746.82
Operating Cost	$14,240.89	$42,722.68
Total Costs	$25,215.89	$54,469.49
Gross Cash	$39,284.11	$25,466.81
Investment (Downpayment)	$15,000.00	$15,000.00
Operating Cost	$14,240.89	$42,722.68
Total Out of Pocket	$29,240.89	$57,722.68
Net Profit	$10,043.21	$(32,255.87)
Return on Investment	34%	−56%

For this worksheet, all the variables and calculated fields are in columns D, E, G, and H. Here is a rundown of the cell content:

D9=D5-(D5*D7)	E23=SUM(D18:D22)
D18=IF(D10,((PMT(D10,D11,D9,0,0))*-1),0)	E28=SUM(D26:D27)
D19=IF(D11,((PMT(D10,D11,D6,0,0))*-1),0)	E31=SUM(D29:D30)
	E32=E28-E31
D20=D12	E35=SUM(D33:D34)
D21=D14	E36=E32-E35
D22=D13	E40=SUM(D38:D39)
D26=H8	E41=E36-E40
D27=(D5*H6)	E42=IF(E41,(E41/E40),0)
D29=D9	H23=SUM(G18:G22)
D30=D6	H28=SUM(G26:G27)
D33=E28*H5	H31=SUM(G29:J30)
D34=E23	H32=H28-H31
D38=D8	H35=SUM(G33:G34)
D39=D34	H36=H32-H35
G18=IF(D10,(((PMT(D10,D11,D9,0,0))*-1)*H7),0)	H40=SUM(G38:G39)
D19=(IF(D11,((PMT(D10,D11,D6,0,0))*-1),0))*H7	H41=H36-H40
	H42=IF(H41,(H41/H40),0)
G20=D12*H7	
G21=D14*H7	
G22=D13*H7	
G26=H8	
G27=((FV(H6,H7,0,H8,0))*-1)-H8	

G29=D9	
G30=D6	
G33=H28*H5	
G34=H23	
G38=D8	
G39=H23	

 You can download these worksheets from the included CD-Rom.

CHAPTER 4

BUYING AND SELLING PROPERTY

Negotiating a buy or sell deal and navigating through the process are intimidating even for a seasoned investor. To help keep the process on track, we've compiled a "Buyer's Checklist" and a "Seller's Checklist" and information about hiring home inspectors. To explain the finer points of settlement statements for buyer and seller, we've enclosed two of them for you to look over. And there's also a blank settlement statement from the U.S. Department of Housing and Urban Development (HUD). By reviewing all the line items on this form, you'll get an idea of the details of the process. By being prepared and knowing the information needed, we hope that you will avoid any loose ends at closing time.

Buyer's and Seller's Checklists

These checklists are designed as crib sheets for buyers or sellers. A good broker should act as a clearinghouse to make sure that all the steps of the process are followed and act as a go-between for you, the loan officer, and the seller's broker. The other key players are the lending or bank officer who handles all the financial aspects involved and lawyers representing the buyer and seller who consummate the deal. Ultimately, however, the buyer and seller have it in their own best interests to make sure that the deal goes down. This may involve following up with any and all of the players to bring the deal to closure on time and with no surprises.

If there is anything you don't understand or question, make your concern known to whomever is best suited to deal with it. For example, if there's a misunderstanding or discrepancy between the closing date and the occupancy date, ask the broker. If the closing statement you review prior to the closing indicates expenditures that you don't understand, call the broker or loan officer before the closing date so that all concerns can be addressed.

Use the "Notes" section of the checklists as guidelines to anticipate the process, expenses, and responsibilities you as a buyer or a seller have so that the closing is a mere formality.

BUYER'S CHECKLIST

There are several tasks required between when an offer is accepted and the property closing. A good broker will act as a clearinghouse for these items, but the buyer and seller are ultimately responsible. If you are the buyer, use this checklist to guide you through the process.

Tasks	Notes
☐ Order a home inspection of the property	
☐ Review issues of inspection with seller	
☐ Confirm and lock in financing	
☐ Review closing-cost estimates	
☐ Order property appraisal	
☐ Order title search	
☐ Order title insurance	
☐ Consult lender about progress of loan	
☐ Order home insurance	
☐ Consult with utility companies about changing names on service records	
☐ Schedule final walk-through	
☐ Review final settlement statement	
☐ Get checks issued for settlement	
☐ Confirm closing date	
☐ Make money transfers to escrow account	
☐ Confirm time address of settlement location	

SELLER'S CHECKLIST

Before you sign a contract to list your property for sale, take the time to make it as desirable and market-ready as you can. Use this checklist to guide you through the sales process.

Tasks	Notes
☐ Define your goal and the right time for selling	
☐ Decide if you will sell it by owner or with a sales agent	
☐ If you are using an agent, ask for a comparative marketing analysis, and review the terms of the listing contract	
☐ If you are selling it yourself, develop a marketing plan	
☐ Go over finances to know the costs involved	
☐ Determine where you're moving to, and begin the process of preparing for the move	
☐ Order a presale inspection of the property	
☐ Make suggested repairs noted on the inspection report	
☐ Schedule a yard sale or the removal of unwanted items	
☐ Remove all garbage, debris, and excess materials	
☐ Complete all cleaning tasks	
☐ Check that home insurance coverage includes the house being on the market	
☐ Order extra set of keys for the sales agent	
☐ Consult with utility companies about changing names on service records	

✔ SELLER'S CHECKLIST	Page 2

Before you sign a contract to list your property for sale, take the time to make it as desirable and market-ready as you can. Use this checklist to guide you through the sales process.

Tasks	Notes
☐ Schedule final walk-through	
☐ Discontinue insurance as of closing date	
☐ Review final settlement statement	
☐ Arrange to make loan payoff with lender	
☐ Arrange to stop service on all utilities in your name and transfer to new owner	
☐ Get address of settlement location	
☐ Make loan payoff to lender	

Buyer's Home Inspection

A home inspection by a professional should give you a thorough evaluation of a house, including its interior and exterior spaces and all the systems running through it. Before hiring a home inspector, go over the buyer's checklist to ensure that you find an inspector whose report will tell you the condition of the structure, systems, and all other aspects of the house.

Since real estate deals hinge on the report from a home inspector, brokers and lenders usually have a list of qualified companies to recommend. In the Yellow Pages, you'll find home inspectors listed under "Building Inspection." On the Internet, you'll find information using any search engine such as Google or Yahoo. Type "home inspector" in the search box, and a list of Web sites of inspection associations and companies will appear. Membership in a national or state trade association means that the inspector has an expertise in home construction and agrees to certain standards of conduct. The sites all feature locator buttons to find one of their members in your area. A typical inspection costs about $500 for a thorough examination of the property with an itemized report of what is found.

A property may require more than a general inspection and need the skills of a specialist. For example, if a house has severe termite damage or hazardous materials such as asbestos or lead paint, call in someone who specializes in the field. For a professional opinion on a historic house, call in an inspector who has experience with historic preservation.

✔ CHECKLIST FOR HIRING A HOME INSPECTOR

☐ Ask the inspector (or inspection company) what his or her (or their) qualifications are. Does the inspector have experience or training in house construction and maintenance? Is he or she a member of a professional organization who has received training?

☐ Get a list of customers with similar homes to the one being inspected so that you can ask for references. Call the references to see if they're satisfied with the results of the inspection.

☐ Find out the scope or extent of the inspection. Will the inspector climb up to the roof to see the shingles? Does the inspection include operating all the appliances and systems of the house?

☐ Ask the cost of a typical inspection, what it includes, and when you'll receive the report.

☐ If you're uncertain about the details covered in the report, ask to see a sample of one for a house similar to yours. A report with a clear description and details is better than one with a simple check-off box. Look for recommendations where a finding or conclusion requires attention or further action.

☐ Can you attend the inspection? If so, go prepared with a list of your questions and concerns, and discuss them as you go through the house. Bring a digital camera or recorder to document what you see and learn.

☐ As you go through the inspection process, ask the inspector to point out problems and recommendations to correct them. Bring a notebook or recorder to have a record of what's said.

☐ Find out if the inspector carries insurance to cover any mistakes he or she makes and if some or all of the structural and mechanical systems of the house are examined.

Settlement Statements

The Department of Housing and Urban Development (HUD) publishes a closing statement that is used for most real estate transactions. This form lists the expenses and adjustments for a typical real estate sale. The statement lists the obligations of the seller in the right column and the purchaser in the left.

For example, in the first Buyer's Statement the purchaser's expense is listed on the left and summarized on the second page. At closing the buyer would have to come up with $3,100 to cover expenses like title insurance, taxes, insurance and transfer fees.

The second example shows what the obligations would be for a seller of a property. The right column lists the cost like real estate commission, prorated taxes and transfer fees associated with this transaction. In this case the seller would have to come up with $28,349.20. This expense is taken out of the proceeds from the sale and the seller does not actually pay out of pocket. But if

A. **Settlement Statement**

U.S. Department of Housing and Urban Development

B. Type of Loan

OMB No. 2502-0265 REV. HUD-1 (3/86)

1. ☐FHA 2. ☐FmHA 3. ☒Conv. Unins.	6. File Number	7. Loan Number	8. Mortgage Insurance Case Number
4. ☐VA 5. ☐Conv. Ins.		**N/A**	**N/A**

C. Note: This form is furnished to give you a statement of actual settlement costs. Amounts paid to and by the settlement agent are shown. Items marked "(p.o.c.)" were paid outside the closing; they are shown here for information purposes and are not included in the totals. WARNING: It is a crime to knowingly make false statements to the United States on this or any other similar form. Penalties upon conviction can include a fine and imprisonment. For details see: Title 18 U. S. Code Section 1001 and Section 1010.

TitleExpress Settlement System
Printed 05/27/2004 at 10:08 NRL

D. NAME OF BORROWER:
  ADDRESS:

E. NAME OF SELLER:
  ADDRESS:

F. NAME OF LENDER:
  ADDRESS:

G. PROPERTY ADDRESS:

H. SETTLEMENT AGENT:
  PLACE OF SETTLEMENT:

I. SETTLEMENT DATE:

J. SUMMARY OF BORROWER'S TRANSACTION:		K. SUMMARY OF SELLER'S TRANSACTION:	
100. GROSS AMOUNT DUE FROM BORROWER		**400. GROSS AMOUNT DUE TO SELLER**	
101. Contract sales price	200,000.00	401. Contract sales price	200,000.00
102. Personal Property		402. Personal Property	
103. Settlement charges to borrower (line 1400)	3,100.00	403.	
104.		404.	
105.		405.	
Adjustments for items paid by seller in advance		Adjustments for items paid by seller in advance	
106. City/town taxes 05/27/04 to 06/30/04	99.07	406. City/town taxes 05/27/04 to 06/30/04	99.07
108. Assessments 05/27/04 to 12/31/04	89.99	408. Assessments 05/27/04 to 12/31/04	89.99
109.		409.	
110.		410.	
111.		411.	
112.		412.	
120. GROSS AMOUNT DUE FROM BORROWER	203,289.06	**420. GROSS AMOUNT DUE TO SELLER**	200,189.06
200. AMOUNTS PAID BY OR ON BEHALF OF BORROWER		**500. REDUCTIONS IN AMOUNT DUE TO SELLER**	
201. Deposit or earnest money	500.00	501. Excess Deposit (see instructions)	500.00
202. Principal amount of new loans		502. Settlement charges to seller (line 1400)	2,120.00
203. Existing loan(s) taken subject to		503. Existing loan(s) taken subject to	
204.		504. Payoff:6643273185	173,610.97
		BANK OF AMERICA	
205.		505. Payoff:68519000982999	26,150.43
		BANK OF AMERICA	
206.		506.	
207.		507.	
208.		508.	
209.		509.	
Adjustments for items unpaid by seller		Adjustments for items unpaid by seller	
213. MARTINGHAM UTILITIES 04/01/04 to 05/27/04	95.73	513. MARTINGHAM UTILITIES 04/01/04 to 05/27/04	95.73
214.		514.	
215.		515.	
216.		516.	
217.		517.	
218.		518.	
219.		519.	
220. TOTAL PAID BY/FOR BORROWER	595.73	**520. TOTAL REDUCTION AMOUNT DUE SELLER**	202,477.13
300. CASH AT SETTLEMENT FROM OR TO BORROWER		**600. CASH AT SETTLEMENT TO OR FROM SELLER**	
301. Gross amount due from borrower (line 120)	203,289.06	601. Gross amount due to seller (line 420)	200,189.06
302. Less amounts paid by/for borrower (line 220)	595.73	602. Less reduction amount due seller (line 520)	202,477.13
303. CASH FROM BORROWER	202,693.33	**603. CASH FROM SELLER**	2,288.07

U.S. DEPARTMENT OF HOUSING AND URBAN DEVELOPMENT   File Number: PAGE 2
SETTLEMENT STATEMENT   REV. HUD-1 (3/86)   TitleExpress Settlement System Printed   .. at

L. SETTLEMENT CHARGES	PAID FROM BORROWER'S FUNDS AT SETTLEMENT	PAID FROM SELLER'S FUNDS AT SETTLEMENT
700. TOTAL SALES/BROKER'S COMMISSION based on price $200,000.00 @ 0.000 =		
Division of commission (line 700) as follows:		
701. $ to		
702. $ to		
703. Commission paid at Settlement		
800. ITEMS PAYABLE IN CONNECTION WITH LOAN		
801. Loan Origination Fee %		
802. Loan Discount %		
803. Appraisal Fee		
804. Credit Report		
805. Lender's Inspection Fee		
806. Mortgage Application Fee		
807. Assumption Fee		
808.		
809.		
810.		
811.		
900. ITEMS REQUIRED BY LENDER TO BE PAID IN ADVANCE		
901. Interest From to @$ /day		
902. Mortgage Insurance Premium for to		
903. Hazard Insurance Premium for to		
904.		
905.		
1000. RESERVES DEPOSITED WITH LENDER FOR		
1001. Hazard Insurance mo. @ $ /mo		
1002. Mortgage Insurance mo. @ $ /mo		
1003. City Property Tax mo. @ $ 86.11 /mo		
1004. County Property Tax mo. @ $ /mo		
1005. Annual Assessments mo. @ $ 52.00 /mo		
1009. Aggregate Analysis Adjustment	0.00	0.00
1100. TITLE CHARGES		
1101. Settlement or closing fee to TITLE COMPANY	375.00	
1102. Abstract or title search		
1103. Title examination		
1104. Title insurance binder to TITLE COMPANY	25.00	
1105. Document Preparation to TITLE COMPANY	50.00	
1106. Notary Fees		
1107. Attorney's fees		
(includes above items No:)		
1108. Title Insurance to **TITLE INSURANCE CORPORATION**	700.00	
(includes above items No:)		
1109. Lender's Policy		
1110. Owner's Policy 200,000.00 - 700.00		
1111.		
1112.		
1113.		
1200. GOVERNMENT RECORDING AND TRANSFER CHARGES		
1201. Recording Fees Deed $ 40.00 ; Mortgage $; Release $	40.00	
1202. State Recordation Tax Deed $1,320.00 ; Mortgage $	660.00	660.00
1203. State Transfer Tax Deed $1,000.00 ; Mortgage $	500.00	500.00
1204. County Transfer Tax Deed $1,500.00 ; Mortgage $	750.00	750.00
1205. RECORD TWO RELEASES to CLERK OF THE CIRCUIT COURT		60.00
1300. ADDITIONAL SETTLEMENT CHARGES		
1301. Survey		
1302. COST ADVANCE COURIER FEE to SHORE TITLE COMPANY		50.00
1303. PROCESS AND PROCURE PAYOFF to SHORE TITLE COMPANY		100.00
1304.		
1305.		
1306.		
1307.		
1308.		
1400. TOTAL SETTLEMENT CHARGES (enter on lines 103, Section J and 502, Section K)	3,100.00	2,120.00

A. Settlement Statement

U.S. Department of Housing and Urban Development

B. Type of Loan

OMB No. 2502-0265 REV. HUD-1 (3/86)

1. ☐FHA 2. ☐FmHA 3. ☒Conv. Unins.	6. File Number	7. Loan Number	8. Mortgage Insurance Case Number
4. ☐VA 5. ☐Conv. Ins.			N/A

C. Note: This form is furnished to give you a statement of actual settlement costs. Amounts paid to and by the settlement agent are shown. Items marked "(p.o.c.)" were paid outside the closing; they are shown here for information purposes and are not included in the totals. WARNING: It is a crime to knowingly make false statements to the United States on this or any other similar form. Penalties upon conviction can include a fine and imprisonment. For details see: Title 18 U. S. Code Section 1001 and Section 1010.

TitleExpress Settlement System

Printed 05/27/2004 at 08:57 NRL

D. NAME OF BORROWER:
  ADDRESS:

E. NAME OF SELLER:
  ADDRESS:

F. NAME OF LENDER:
  ADDRESS:

G. PROPERTY ADDRESS:

H. SETTLEMENT AGENT:
  PLACE OF SETTLEMENT:

I. SETTLEMENT DATE: 05/27/2004

J. SUMMARY OF BORROWER'S TRANSACTION:		K. SUMMARY OF SELLER'S TRANSACTION:	
100. GROSS AMOUNT DUE FROM BORROWER		**400. GROSS AMOUNT DUE TO SELLER**	
101. Contract sales price	399,000.00	401. Contract sales price	399,000.00
102. Personal Property		402. Personal Property	
103. Settlement charges to borrower (line 1400)	7,390.40	403.	
104.		404.	
105.		405.	
Adjustments for items paid by seller in advance		*Adjustments for items paid by seller in advance*	
106. City/town taxes 05/27/04 to 06/30/04	258.81	406. City/town taxes 05/27/04 to 06/30/04	258.81
108. Assessments 05/27/04 to 06/30/04	22.05	408. Assessments 05/27/04 to 06/30/04	22.05
109. TALBOT CTY BENEFIT 05/27/04 to 06/30/04	19.94	409. TALBOT CTY BENEFIT 05/27/04 to 06/30/04	19.94
110.		410.	
111.		411.	
112.		412.	
120. GROSS AMOUNT DUE FROM BORROWER	406,691.20	**420. GROSS AMOUNT DUE TO SELLER**	399,300.80
200. AMOUNTS PAID BY OR ON BEHALF OF BORROWER		**500. REDUCTIONS IN AMOUNT DUE TO SELLER**	
201. Deposit or earnest money	2,000.00	501. Excess Deposit (see instructions)	
202. Principal amount of new loans	250,000.00	502. Settlement charges to seller (line 1400)	28,349.20
203. Existing loan(s) taken subject to		503. Existing loan(s) taken subject to	
204.		504. Payoff:6815417	79,798.87
		MERCANTILE MORTGAGE, LLC	
205.		505.	
206.		506.	
207.		507.	
208.		508.	
209.		509.	
Adjustments for items unpaid by seller		*Adjustments for items unpaid by seller*	
213.		513.	
214.		514.	
215.		515.	
216. Water to 5/27/04	31.35	516. Water to 5/27/04	31.35
217.		517.	
218.		518.	
219.		519.	
220. TOTAL PAID BY/FOR BORROWER	252,031.35	**520. TOTAL REDUCTION AMOUNT DUE SELLER**	108,179.42
300. CASH AT SETTLEMENT FROM OR TO BORROWER		**600. CASH AT SETTLEMENT TO OR FROM SELLER**	
301. Gross amount due from borrower (line 120)	406,691.20	601. Gross amount due to seller (line 420)	399,300.80
302. Less amounts paid by/for borrower (line 220)	252,031.35	602. Less reduction amount due seller (line 520)	108,179.42
303. CASH FROM BORROWER	154,659.85	**603. CASH TO SELLER**	291,121.38

U.S. DEPARTMENT OF HOUSING AND URBAN DEVELOPMENT | File Number: | PAGE 2

SETTLEMENT STATEMENT   REV. HUD-1 (3/86)   TitleExpress Settlement System   Printed

L. SETTLEMENT CHARGES	PAID FROM BORROWER'S FUNDS AT SETTLEMENT	PAID FROM SELLER'S FUNDS AT SETTLEMENT
700. TOTAL SALES/BROKER'S COMMISSION based on price $399,000.00 @ 6.000 = 23,940.00		
Division of commission (line 700) as follows:		
701. $ 11,970.00 to BENSON & MANGOLD		
702. $ 11,970.00 to RE/MAX BLAKENEY LLC		
703. Commission paid at Settlement		23,940.00
800. ITEMS PAYABLE IN CONNECTION WITH LOAN		
801. Loan Origination Fee %		
802. Loan Discount %		
803. Appraisal Fee to **Appraiser** (P.O.C.) 325.00 Buyer		
804. Credit Report to **Broker**	20.00	
805. Tax Service Fee to **COASTAL CAPITAL CORP.**	85.00	
806. Loan Review Fee to **COASTAL CAPITAL CORP.**	420.00	
807. Flood Certification Fee to **COASTAL CAPITAL CORP.**	23.00	
808. Courier Fee to **COASTAL CAPITAL CORP.**	100.00	
809.		
810.		
811.		
900. ITEMS REQUIRED BY LENDER TO BE PAID IN ADVANCE		
901. Interest From 05/27/2004 to 06/01/2004 @$ 40.2400 /day 5 Days	201.20	
902. Mortgage Insurance Premium for to		
903. Hazard Insurance Premium for to		
904.		
905.		
1000. RESERVES DEPOSITED WITH LENDER FOR		
1001. Hazard Insurance 3 mo. @ $ /mo		
1002. Mortgage Insurance mo. @ $ /mo		
1003. City Property Tax 2 mo. @ $ /mo		
1004. County Property Tax mo. @ $ /mo		
1005. Annual Assessments mo. @ $ /mo		
1009.	0.00	0.00
1100. TITLE CHARGES		
1101. Settlement or closing fee to **EASTERN SHORE TITLE COMPANY**	375.00	
1102. Abstract or title search		
1103. Title examination		
1104. Title insurance binder to **TITLE COMPANY**	25.00	
1105. Document Preparation to **TITLE COMPANY**	50.00	
1106. Notary Fees		
1107. Attorney's fees		
(includes above items No:)		
1108. Title Insurance to **SECURITY TITLE GUARANTEE CORPORATION**	1,357.00	
(includes above items No:)		
1109. Lender's Policy 250,000.00 - 625.00		
1110. Owner's Policy 399,000.00 - 732.00		
1111.		
1112.		
1113.		
1200. GOVERNMENT RECORDING AND TRANSFER CHARGES		
1201. Recording Fees Deed $ 40.00 ; Mortgage $ 95.00 ; Release $	135.00	
1202. State Recordation Tax Deed $2,633.40 ; Mortgage $	1,316.70	1,316.70
1203. State Transfer Tax Deed $1,995.00 ; Mortgage $	997.50	997.50
1204. County Transfer Tax Deed $3,990.00 ; Mortgage $	1,995.00	1,995.00
1205. RECORD RELEASE to **CLERK OF THE CIRCUIT COURT**		30.00
1300. ADDITIONAL SETTLEMENT CHARGES		
1301. Survey to ' **SURVEYORS**	175.00	
1302. Pest Inspection to **TERMITE & PEST CONTROL**	65.00	
1303. COSTS ADVANCED - COURIER to **TITLE COMPANY**	50.00	20.00
1304. Procure and Process to **TITLE COMPANY**		50.00
1305.		
1306.		
1307.		
1308.		
1400. TOTAL SETTLEMENT CHARGES (enter on lines 103, Section J and 502, Section K)	7,390.40	28,349.20

A. Settlement Statement

U.S. Department of Housing
and Urban Development

OMB Approval No. 2502-0265
(expires 11/30/2009)

B. Type of Loan

1. ☐ FHA 2. ☐ FmHA 3. ☐ Conv. Unins.	6. File Number:
4. ☐ VA 5. ☐ Conv. Ins.	7. Loan Number:
	8. Mortgage Insurance Case Number:

C. Note: This form is furnished to give you a statement of actual settlement costs. Amounts paid to and by the settlement agent are shown. Items marked "(p.o.c.)" were paid outside the closing; they are shown here for informational purposes and are not included in the totals.

D. Name & Address of Borrower:	E. Name & Address of Seller:	F. Name & Address of Lender:

G. Property Location:	H. Settlement Agent:
	Place of Settlement:	I. Settlement Date:

J. Summary of Borrower's Transaction		**K. Summary of Seller's Transaction**	
100. Gross Amount Due From Borrower		**400. Gross Amount Due To Seller**	
101. Contract sales price		401. Contract sales price	
102. Personal property		402. Personal property	
103. Settlement charges to borrower (line 1400)		403.	
104.		404.	
105.		405.	
Adjustments for items paid by seller in advance		**Adjustments for items paid by seller in advance**	
106. City/town taxes to		406. City/town taxes to	
107. County taxes to		407. County taxes to	
108. Assessments to		408. Assessments to	
109.		409.	
110.		410.	
111.		411.	
112.		412.	
120. Gross Amount Due From Borrower		**420. Gross Amount Due To Seller**	
200. Amounts Paid By Or In Behalf Of Borrower		**500. Reductions In Amount Due To Seller**	
201. Deposit or earnest money		501. Excess deposit (see instructions)	
202. Principal amount of new loan(s)		502. Settlement charges to seller (line 1400)	
203. Existing loan(s) taken subject to		503. Existing loan(s) taken subject to	
204.		504. Payoff of first mortgage loan	
205.		505. Payoff of second mortgage loan	
206.		506.	
207.		507.	
208.		508.	
209.		509.	
Adjustments for items unpaid by seller		**Adjustments for items unpaid by seller**	
210. City/town taxes to		510. City/town taxes to	
211. County taxes to		511. County taxes to	
212. Assessments to		512. Assessments to	
213.		513.	
214.		514.	
215.		515.	
216.		516.	
217.		517.	
218.		518.	
219.		519.	
220. Total Paid By/For Borrower		**520. Total Reduction Amount Due Seller**	
300. Cash At Settlement From/To Borrower		**600. Cash At Settlement To/From Seller**	
301. Gross Amount due from borrower (line 120)		601. Gross amount due to seller (line 420)	
302. Less amounts paid by/for borrower (line 220)	( )	602. Less reductions in amt. due seller (line 520)	( )
303. Cash ☐ From ☐ To Borrower		**603. Cash** ☐ To ☐ From Seller	

Section 5 of the Real Estate Settlement Procedures Act (RESPA) requires the following: • HUD must develop a Special Information Booklet to help persons borrowing money to finance the purchase of residential real estate to better understand the nature and costs of real estate settlement services; • Each lender must provide the booklet to all applicants from whom it receives or for whom it prepares a written application to borrow money to finance the purchase of residential real estate; • Lenders must prepare and distribute with the Booklet a Good Faith Estimate of the settlement costs that the borrower is likely to incur in connection with the settlement. These disclosures are manadatory.

Section 4(a) of RESPA mandates that HUD develop and prescribe this standard form to be used at the time of loan settlement to provide full disclosure of all charges imposed upon the borrower and seller. These are third party disclosures that are designed to provide the borrower with pertinent information during the settlement process in order to be a better shopper.

The Public Reporting Burden for this collection of information is estimated to average one hour per response, including the time for reviewing instructions, searching existing data sources, gathering and maintaining the data needed, and completing and reviewing the collection of information.

This agency may not collect this information, and you are not required to complete this form, unless it displays a currently valid OMB control number.

The information requested does not lend itself to confidentiality.

Previous editions are obsolete

Page 1 of 2

form **HUD-1** (3/86)
ref Handbook 4305.2

L. Settlement Charges

		Paid From Borrowers Funds at Settlement	Paid From Seller's Funds at Settlement
700. Total Sales/Broker's Commission based on price $ @ % =			
Division of Commission (line 700) as follows:			
701. $ to			
702. $ to			
703. Commission paid at Settlement			
704.			
800. Items Payable In Connection With Loan			
801. Loan Origination Fee %			
802. Loan Discount %			
803. Appraisal Fee to			
804. Credit Report to			
805. Lender's Inspection Fee			
806. Mortgage Insurance Application Fee to			
807. Assumption Fee			
808.			
809.			
810.			
811.			
900. Items Required By Lender To Be Paid In Advance			
901. Interest from to @$ /day			
902. Mortgage Insurance Premium for months to			
903. Hazard Insurance Premium for years to			
904. years to			
905.			
1000. Reserves Deposited With Lender			
1001. Hazard insurance months@$ per month			
1002. Mortgage insurance months@$ per month			
1003. City property taxes months@$ per month			
1004. County property taxes months@$ per month			
1005. Annual assessments months@$ per month			
1006. months@$ per month			
1007. months@$ per month			
1008. months@$ per month			
1100. Title Charges			
1101. Settlement or closing fee to			
1102. Abstract or title search to			
1103. Title examination to			
1104. Title insurance binder to			
1105. Document preparation to			
1106. Notary fees to			
1107. Attorney's fees to			
(includes above items numbers:)			
1108. Title insurance to			
(includes above items numbers:)			
1109. Lender's coverage $			
1110. Owner's coverage $			
1111.			
1112.			
1113.			
1200. Government Recording and Transfer Charges			
1201. Recording fees: Deed $; Mortgage $; Releases $			
1202. City/county tax/stamps: Deed $; Mortgage $			
1203. State tax/stamps: Deed $; Mortgage $			
1204.			
1205.			
1300. Additional Settlement Charges			
1301. Survey to			
1302. Pest inspection to			
1303.			
1304.			
1305.			
1400. Total Settlement Charges (enter on lines 103, Section J and 502, Section K)			

The Undersigned Acknowledges Receipt of this Disclosure Statement and Agrees to the Correctness Thereof.

_____   _____

_____   _____

Buyer or Agent   Seller or Agent

the money generated by the sale was less than this figure the seller would have to make up the difference. If the seller paid close to $300,000 for the house this could be a difficult transaction for the seller.

We have included a blank closing statement that you can use to estimate the many costs that will come due when you purchase or sell a property.

 You can download these checklists and settlement statements from the included CD-Rom.

CHAPTER 5

ESTIMATING FIX-UP COSTS

T he cost of the job—this is what you need to consider when it comes to making an accurate estimate of improvements to a property. The calculators in this chapter show you how to calculate the amount of material to purchase to help you control your cost.

A contractor comes up with an estimate for a specific project based on his or her experience with past jobs. If the contractor keeps good payroll records, he or she knows the labor costs to perform specific jobs, and he or she knows the local cost of skilled labor such as carpenters, electricians, and plumbers. The contractor calls local suppliers to get the latest materials cost and sits down to compile a bid.

Many pros rely on materials and labor cost data compiled by major publishers such as the R. S. Means Company and the Craftsman Book Company to help put together their bids. These publishers have been collecting construction cost data and compiling them into books and software for years. You can purchase these books and use them to make accurate estimates of how much your planned renovations will cost. Also, you can use Craftsman Book Company's National Home Improvement Estimator at the company's Web site www.get-a-quote.net. There you will find a listing of materials and labor costs for hundreds of jobs.

We invite you to use our Web site www.diyornot.com to find the cost of more than 300 specific projects. Just choose a project from the categories and type in your zip code in the "Cost Box" to find the regional cost of a project, both the cost of doing it yourself and the cost of hiring a contractor in your area.

On the CD-Rom you will find the calculators in this section.

Painting Calculators

Just about every renovation involves some sort of painting. Following are a series of paint calculator worksheets to allow you to accurately figure the amount of paint you will need. To use these worksheets, you will need the dimensions of the room and the number of doors and windows.

Since paint coverage per gallon is figured in gallons per square foot, measure in feet. For example, for a 36-inch-wide window, you would use 3 feet for its width in the worksheet. Extreme accuracy is not necessary in these measurements because the amount of paint will be rounded off to the nearest gallon or quart. In fact, depending on the cost of the paint, it is usually cheaper to purchase an extra gallon if you need more than a couple of quarts.

Another factor affecting the amount of paint you will need is the type of surface you are painting. For example, new, unpainted drywall is very porous and absorbs a large amount of paint into the paper facing. You will not get the same coverage per gallon as if you were painting a prepainted wall. Texture also affects paint coverage. You must use a heavy-nap roller (very fuzzy) to work the paint into a textured ceiling or wall surface, and this requires more paint. To allow for this, you will see two different coverage factors on the worksheets. Look for the manufacturer's recommended coverage that is printed on the paint's label can.

The wall and ceiling worksheets use the same logic: paintable area divided by the paint per gallon coverage factor. Here is an example on how you can use the "Wall Paint Worksheet" to calculate the amount of paint needed to paint a 10- by 12-foot room with 8-foot ceilings and two standard doors and a window.

First you add up the length of the walls, which is $10 + 12 + 10 + 12 = 44$ feet. The ceiling height is 8 feet, so the area is $44 \times 8 = 352$ square feet.

Next, you find the area of the window glass that will not be painted. You can use 15 square feet per standard window or calculate the area as $3 \times 5 = 15$ square feet.

The doors are figured in the same way. The standard allowance for a door is 21 square feet per door, and we have an entrance door and a closet door, so fill in the worksheet like this: $3 \times 7 = 21 \times 2 = 42$ square feet.

The area that we will have to paint is the wall area minus the window and door areas, so the fill in the worksheet like this: $352 - 15 - 42 = 295$ square feet.

Since we are painting a smooth surface, we then divide the paintable area by the coverage factor and get $294/450 = 0.66$ gallon. Because this is more than

Wall Paint Calculator

Wall Area
[+   +   +   ] × [   ] = [   ]
Total Length of All Walls   Wall Height   Wall Area

Window Area
[   ] × [   ] = [   ] × [   ] = [   ]
    Height   Width   Area   # of Windows   Window Area

Door Area
[   ] × [   ] = [   ] × [   ] = [   ]
    Height   Width   Area   # of Doors   Door Area

Paintable Area
[   ] − [   ] − [   ] = [   ]
    Wall Area   Window Area   Door Area   Paintable Area

Paint to Order
[   ] / [   ] = [   ]
 Paintable Area   Coverage   Gallons
Smooth-Surface Coverage = 450
Rough-Surface Coverage = 350

Ceiling Paint Calculator

[   ] × [   ] = [   ]
    Room Length   Room Width   Ceiling Area

Paint to Order
[   ] / [   ] = [   ]
    Ceiling Area   Coverage   Gallons
Smooth-Surface Coverage = 450
Rough-Surface Coverage = 350

Window Paint Calculator

Window Area
[   ] × [   ] = [   ] × [   ] = [   ]
    Height   Width   Area   # of Windows   Area

Paintable Area
[   ] × [   ] = [   ]
    Window Area   Coverage   Paintable Area

Paint to Order
[   ] / [   ] = [   ]
  Paintable Area   Coverage   Gallons

Door Paint Calculator

Door Area
[   ] × [   ] = [   ] × [   ] = [   ]
    Door Height   Door Width   Door Area   # of Doors   Door Area

Paintable Area
[   ] × [   ] = [   ]
    Door Area   Sides to Paint   Paintable Area

Paint to Order
[   ] / [   ] = [   ]
  Paintable Area   Coverage   Gallons

a half gallon, we would suggest that you purchase a gallon of wall paint for this project.

The window and door worksheets take into consideration the areas not painted and subtract them from the total area to get the paintable area. Basically, it's the glass area of the window and door, if any, that is not painted. But these areas have cross-members called *rails* and *styles* that need paint. Therefore, depending on the type of window or door, the actual glass area may be small. Remember that both sides of these dividers need to be painted. For example, a plate glass window may have over 70 percent glass compared with a window with many divided lights or small panes with only 30 percent glass.

Wallpaper Calculator

Figuring the amount of wallpaper to purchase can get a bit tricky. The area to wallpaper is calculated just like a paintable wall surface, but all rolls of wallpaper are not created alike. You will find wallpaper in either American or European rolls that have different coverage, and some rolls are sold as *double rolls* even though they're in a single package.

In addition, the wallpaper's pattern can dramatically affect the amount of usable paper, called the *yield*, that you can expect to get from a roll. The larger the pattern or pattern repeat, the more paper must be wasted to match the pattern from strip to strip. For example, if the paper has a 12-inch pattern repeat, in order to match the paper pattern to the adjoining strip, the next strip may have to be moved up a foot or so to align the two patterns. In this case, the top of the paper will be trimmed away and be wasted.

This worksheet uses the same method to determine the area to be papered as the "Wall Paint Calculator." Once you know the area you want to cover with paper, you adjust this figure for some unavoidable waste. Unless you are an experienced paperhanger, use the default waste figure of 20 percent. In other words, each roll will cover only 80 percent of its stated coverage, so you multiply the coverage by 0.80.

For example, if you choose a paper in an American roll with a pattern repeat of 7 to 12 inches, you would use 30 square feet as the roll coverage. Enter this figure in the "Roll Coverage" variable, and then multiply this figure by 0.80 to get the adjusted coverage. Then divide the area by the adjusted coverage to get the number of rolls to order.

There is another factor to consider: Wallpaper is manufactured in batches. Make sure that all the rolls you purchase are from the same batch. Check the batch number that is marked on each roll, and make sure that they all match. You may want to purchase a couple of extra rolls just to be on the safe side; ask

Wallpaper Calculator

Wall Area
[+   +   +   +   ] × [   ] = [   ]
 Length of All Walls   Wall Height   Wall Area

Window Area
[   ] × [   ] = [   ]
 Window Height   Window Width   Window Area

Door Area
[   ] × [   ] = [   ]
 Door Height   Door Width   Door Area

Area to Wallpaper
[   ] – [   ] – [   ] = [   ]
 Wall Area   Window Area   Door Area   Wallpaper Area

Waste Adjustment
[   ] × [0.80] = [   ]
 Roll Coverage   Adjusted Coverage

Wallpaper Rolls to Order
[   ]/[   ] = [   ]
 Area   Adjusted Coverage   # of Rolls

Usable Yield Chart

American Rolls		European Rolls	
Pattern Repeat (Drop)	Usable Yield	Pattern Repeat (Drop)	Usable Yield
0–6 inches	32 square feet	0–6 inches	25 square feet
7–12 inches	30 square feet	7–12 inches	22 square feet
13–18 inches	27 square feet	13–18 inches	20 square feet
19–23 inches	25 square feet	19–23 inches	18 square feet

when ordering if unopened rolls can be returned. You also may want to keep one for later repairs.

Wallboard Calculator

Calculating drywall is very straightforward because you don't put drywall over doors or windows—the area to cover is the same as with painting ceilings or walls. The only other factor to consider is the length of the sheets. Whenever possible, use the 12-foot-long sheet because this produces fewer joints.

The other factor to consider is that the smaller the job, the higher is the waste factor. Also, any area with curved or angular walls will add to the waste.

Tile Calculator

Unless you use 12-inch-square tiles, the amount of tiles required to cover a square foot of area must be adjusted by a coverage factor. If the tiles are smaller

Wallboard Calculator

Wall Area

[+ + +] × [   ] = [   ]
  Total Length of All Walls   Wall Height   Wall Area

Wall Area

[   ] × [   ] = [   ] × [   ] = [   ]
  Window Height   Window Width   Window Area   # of Windows   Window Area

[   ] × [   ] = [   ] × [   ] = [   ]
  Door Height   Door Width   Door Area   # of Doors   Door Area

[   ] − [   ] − [   ] = [   ]
  Wall Area   Window Area   Door Area   Wall Area

Wallboard Sheets to Order

[   ] / [   ] = [   ]
  Wall Area   Coverage   Sheets

4 × 8 ft Sheet coverage = 32
4 × 12 ft Sheet Coverage = 48

Tile Calculator

[   ] × [   ] / [   ] = Tiles to Purchase
  Length   Width   Coverage

4-inch Tiles: Coverage = 0.1089   12-inch Tiles: Coverage = 1
6-inch Tiles: Coverage = 0.25   18-inch Tiles: Coverage = 2.25
9-inch Tiles: Coverage = 0.5625

Carpet Calculator

[   ] × [   ] / [   ] = [   ]
  Length   Width   Coverage   Carpet

Sold by the Square Yard: Coverage = 9 square feet
12-inch Carpet Tiles: Coverage = 1 square foot
18-inch Carpet Tiles: Coverage = 2.25 square feet

Vinyl Floor Calculator

Sheet

[   ] × [   ] = [   ]
  Room Length   Room Width   Flooring Needed

Tile

[   ] / [   ] = [   ]
  Floor Area   Coverage   Tiles

9-inch Tiles: Coverage = 0.5625 square foot
12-inch Tiles: Coverage = 1 square foot

than a square foot, such as a standard 4-inch tile, then you will need more than one to cover the area. For example, a 3- by 6-foot backsplash area covered with standard 4-inch tiles would be calculated like this: $3 \times 6 = 18/0.1089 = 165.28$ tiles. The same area covered with 9-inch tiles would be calculated like this: $3 \times 6 = 18/0.25 = 72$ tiles.

Carpet Calculator

Carpet is sold by the square foot or square yard. Carpet also is available as carpet tiles in varying sizes. Use the coverage factors to adjust the square foot area calculated. For example, if you want to carpet a 12- by 15-foot room and the carpet is sold by the square yard, you would enter these numbers: $12 \times 15 = 180/9 = 20$. This is 20 yards of carpet. Depending on the width of the particular carpet you order, there may be other factors to consider. Before you order carpet, consult with the carpet store.

Vinyl Flooring Calculator

Vinyl flooring is available in both sheet goods, usually sold by the square foot, and 12-inch tiles. If the sheet goods are sold by the square yard, then the area should be divided by 9 to get square yards. Make sure that you know how the sheet goods are quoted, and tell the pro where you order the material the dimensions of the room.

CHAPTER 6

SPACE-EXPANDING POSSIBILITIES

In a house the attic, basement, and porch are the most popular and inexpensive areas with potential for expansion because they are already part of the structure. An attic has an existing roof and floor, a basement is enclosed and often heated, and a porch is an unfinished annex just waiting to be enclosed. However, there are a number of limiting factors. Attic joists and framing may be too lightweight to withstand the load of additional living space. A basement may be plagued with dampness. And an open porch may add more architectural character and value to the house than an additional enclosed space. Use the worksheets in this chapter to take everything into account.

Today, kitchens and bathrooms are the most often remodeled rooms in a house. At one end of the spectrum, these spaces are being updated with simple cosmetic facelifts; at the other extreme, they reinvent themselves in eye-popping transformations. To whatever extent you're planning to remodel, use the worksheets in this chapter to guide you through the process.

STAGES OF BATHROOM—KITCHEN REMODEL

Snapshot of remodeling stages for a kitchen or bathroom. Use this checklist as a reference to plan and execute the project.

- ☐ Budget
- ☐ Planning
- ☐ Shopping
- ☐ Select materials
- ☐ Design and layout
- ☐ Permits

Do-it-yourself or pro

- ☐ Schedule the job and do it yourself
- ☐ Find and hire subcontractors
- ☐ Place orders for materials
- ☐ Demolish and prep

Rough-ins

- ☐ Framing
- ☐ Plumbing
- ☐ Electricals

Inspection of rough-ins

- ☐ Framing
- ☐ Plumbing
- ☐ Electricals

New surfaces

- ☐ Walls
- ☐ Windows
- ☐ Doors
- ☐ Cabinetry
- ☐ Countertop
- ☐ Sinks
- ☐ Flooring
- ☐ Wallcovering
- ☐ Fixtures and hookups
- ☐ Appliances and hookups
- ☐ Final inspection
- ☐ Finishing touches

Kitchen Worksheet Instructions

The busiest room in a house serves up more than meals. It's often tasked with other duties, such as a message center for the household, a homework area for kids, or the centerpiece of the whole house where everyone congregates. To remodel such a pivotal place in a house takes more than careful planning. It requires a lot of time and effort to flush out the options to create a new kitchen. You're in luck when no surprises are found behind old cabinets and no new problems arise when the wrong countertop arrives.

While a kitchen is larger than a bathroom, the same cast of craftspeople is involved: plumbers to handle the water supply for all the fixtures and electricians to power the room with light, ventilation, outlets, and appliances. When the behind-the-walls work is done, the finishers come to install drywall, set tile and solid surfaces, and hang cabinets, and then the painters and paper hangers to finish the job.

The challenge is coordinating these craftspeople so that all phases of the job run smoothly. A kitchen designer or contractor may be hired to do the work, but it is the property owner who is ultimately responsible to make things happen. If the owner is doing some or all of the work, it's essential for him or her to control the project.

The "Kitchen Worksheet" is designed for planning and coordinating such a major makeover. Use it as a guideline to follow, and take the time necessary to review all your options, including reusing some of what's there and redefining the layout of the room. Jot down your thoughts, concerns, and reminders in the "Notes" section, and use the "Image" area when you need a visual reference. Make a rough drawing of the space and floorplan with dimensions so that you'll have quick access to them.

KITCHEN WORKSHEET		
	NOTES	Image Recorder Reference
Determine a budget		
Dimensioned drawing with location of fixtures		
Permits (if necessary)		
Decide/order materials and appliances		
Cabinetry: reuse as is, refinish, or replace		
Sink and countertop: reuse or replace		
Design and lay out a plan		
Do-it-yourself or pro		
Pro interviews		
Decide disposal strategy		
Take down: remove everything and clear area		
Framing rough-in work		
Plumbing rough-in work		
Inspection		
Electrical rough-in work		
Inspection		
Doors		
Windows		
Walls/ceiling		
Install lighting		
Install ventilation		
Flooring		
Hook up plumbing fixtures, appliances		
Hook up electrical fixtures, appliances		
Final inspection		
Wall coverings		
Install accessories		
Other issues		

Sketch kitchen floor plan:

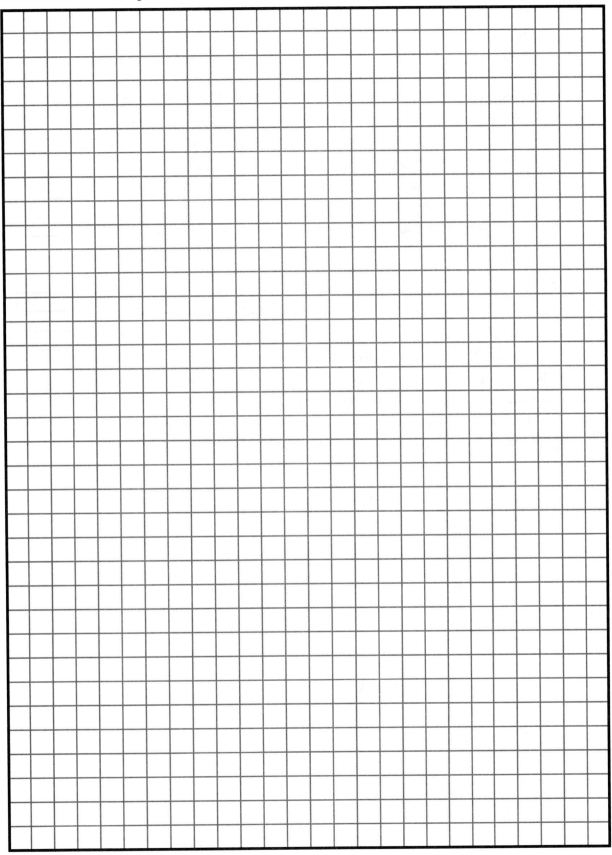

Bathroom Worksheet Instructions

To pull off a successful bathroom remodel, it takes the skills and talents of many individuals, not the least of which is the person managing the project. In one, often small room, just about every major system is involved. Plumbers are the linchpins who deal with water supply for all the fixtures. The skills of electricians are essential for powering the room with light, ventilation, and outlets. Carpenters, drywall contractors, tile and solid-surface installers, and painters and wallpaper hangers add to the list of skilled workers involved.

The challenge is coordinating these craftspeople so that there's no down time when the bathroom sits idle. A bathroom design firm or contractor may be hired to do the work, but the property owner should have a handle on the process. If the owner is doing some or all of the work, it's essential that he or she control the project. This is where the "Bathroom Worksheet" will come in handy. If you're paying someone to do the job, use the worksheet to follow the progress; if you're doing it yourself, the worksheet will help you to manage and coordinate your effort.

Use the "Notes" section to remind you to order a part, make a repair, or call a building inspector—whatever the project requires. The "Image or Recorder Reference" may help you to find a visual when you need one. Use the "Sketch" area to make an overview of the room so that you'll have the dimensions accessible.

BATHROOM WORKSHEET		
	NOTES	Image Recorder Reference
Determine a budget		
Dimensioned drawing with location of fixtures		
Permits (if necessary)		
Decide to reuse or replace fixtures: sink, toilet, tub, shower		
Decide to reuse or replace fittings: faucets, tub-shower valve		
Decide to reuse or replace cabinetry: vanity, countertop, medicine cabinet, built-ins, mirrors		
Design and lay out a plan		
Who does the work: yourself or pro		
Pro interviews		
Decide/order materials and fixtures		
Decide disposal strategy		
Take down: remove everything that goes and clear area		
Framing rough-in work		
Plumbing rough-in work Inspection		
Electrical rough-in work		

BATHROOM WORKSHEET		Page 2
	NOTES	Image Recorder Reference
Inspection		
Doors		
Windows		
Walls/ceiling		
Install cabinets or reuse		
Install lighting		
Install ventilation		
Install fixtures		
Flooring		
Hook up plumbing fixtures		
Hook up electrical fixtures		
Final inspection		
Wall coverings		
Install accessories		
Other issues		

Sketch bathroom floor plan:

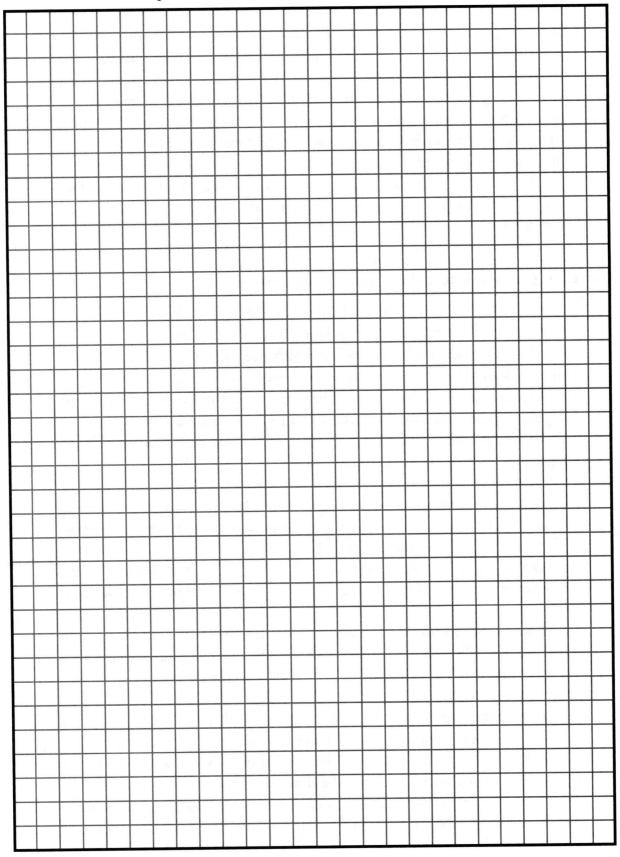

Basement Worksheet Instructions

Improving a basement doesn't require expensive foundation work or building exterior walls like an addition. You can take advantage of what a basement has to offer—walls, ceiling, and a floor—and transform it into usable space, whether it gets a quick paint job and is destined strictly for storage or goes through a major transformation as living space. Use the "Basement Worksheet" to help you to decide how to reuse and redefine the space, and make a sketch of its layout for future reference.

For any project in a basement, moisture is the issue. Moisture in any form is a key deterrent to creating usable storage and living space, so look for condensation, water marks, and signs of seepage on the floor and walls.

For Living Space There Are Many More Issues

Most building codes require a ceiling height of at least 90 inches, which is 7½ feet. A suspended ceiling may be a solution that conceals exposed heating ducts, plumbing lines, and electrical wires, and such a ceiling comes in handy because the panels can be removed for servicing those items.

On your sketch of the basement, be sure to note the location of stack pipes and support poles that can interfere with a room design. Stairs and their location can be another concern for traffic flow. Code-wise check your local building requirement for their size requirements.

Windows and doors are a concern. Windows let daylight in, but they can create a security breach if the glass can be broken. If there is no outside exit from a basement, an egress window—one large enough for a person to get out of in an emergency—often is required.

Get an estimate from a heating, ventilation, and air-conditioning (HVAC) contractor to find out if the existing system can be extended for use in the basement.

Look at the electrical wiring and note if it is grounded or shows any signs of damage or splices. Be concerned about wires that go nowhere. Note the location of lighting fixtures and their switches. Talk to an electrician about upgrading the system for living space.

Inspect the plumbing lines to see if they are galvanized steel, copper, or plastic, and notice how the lines are connected and secured to ceiling rafters. Find the main water line and see if there is a shut-off valve, a check valve, or an antibackflow device. Look for the drain lines that take water out of the house, and notice how they are connected. Also look for signs of leaks. Look at the sump pump, and trip the float rod to test it. When you lift the float, the motor should start.

BASEMENT WORKSHEET		
	NOTES	Image Recorder Reference
Exterior stairwell		
Drain		
Condition of stairs or access		
Window wells		
Free of water and debris		
Foundation and walls		
Signs of seepage through cracks		
Efflorescence (white powdery residue)		
Mold or mildew		
Interior stairs		
Secure handrail		
5-inch or less gap between vertical balusters		
Open or closed stair treads and risers		
Floor		
Cracks in cement floor or slab		
Sump pump		
Free of water and debris		
Put float rod to test		
Ceiling joists		
Signs of rot or pest infestation		
Electrical panel and wiring		
Amperage/voltage rating		
No. of circuits; limited or expandable		

BASEMENT WORKSHEET		Page 2
	NOTES	Image Recorder Reference
Grounded wires		
Wires that go nowhere		
Spliced or damaged wires		
GFCIs		
Grounded outlets		
Lighting fixtures		
Location and switches		
Plumbing lines		
Type of water lines (copper, plastic, galvanized)		
How the lines are connected		
How the lines are secured to ceiling rafters (metal strapping)		
Main water line		
Location		
Shut-off valve		
Check valve or antibackflow device		
Drain lines		
Locations		
How they are connected		
Signs of leaks		
Other issues		

Sketch basement floor plan:

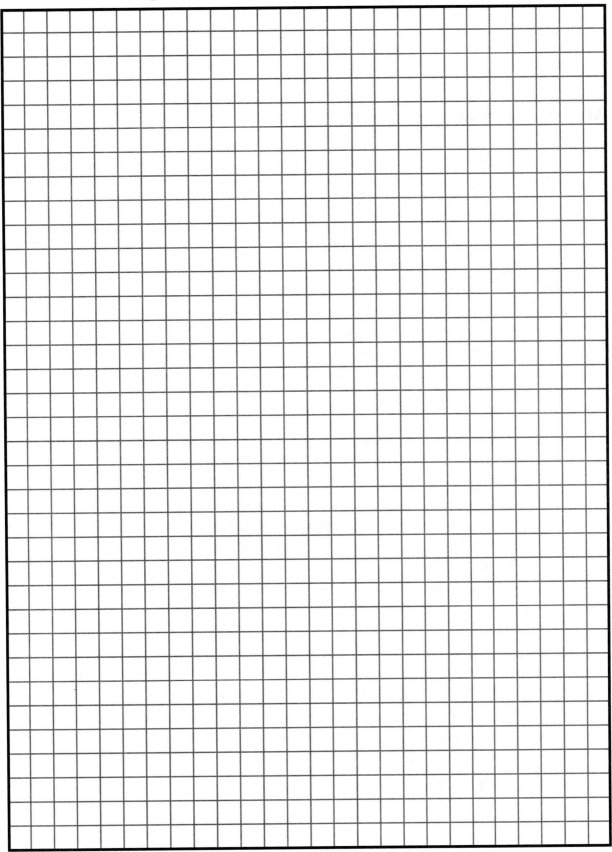

Look at the exposed joists in the ceiling for signs of rot or pest infestation. Termites are a potential problem in most parts of the United States. A professional termite inspection is required in many parts of the country in order to get financing.

Attic Worksheet Instructions

An unfinished attic can be found space because converting it takes advantage of the existing walls, windows, stairs, roof, and siding. To evaluate how best to use the space, take a look at its structure using the "Attic Worksheet" on a clipboard. Make a rough sketch of the attic space to use as a reference. Have a flashlight and long measuring tape handy as you make a thorough walk-through. Use the findings to determine if you can use the attic for storage or living space based on the code requirements.

Look at the attic ceiling or sheathing (the underside of the roof) for signs of any sagging areas and damage from insects, rot, or condensation. Pay particular attention to roof penetrations such as the plumbing vent and chimney, where leaks may occur. Note the type of insulation and if it should be increased for energy conservation.

Generally, if the attic floor has 2- by 6-inch joists or larger joists and the span between the load-bearing walls on the floor below does not exceed 10 to 12 feet, the floor is strong enough to support a living area. But talk to the local building department to find out what's required in your area.

The location of the stairs is a prime factor that determines whether an attic has living space potential; so is the width and depth of stair treads. Take measurements. Headroom is also important. It must be no less than 80 inches, measured vertically from the finished floor at the landings.

Also check the location of the plumbing soil stack as it leads up through the roof to vent the system. This will be the most economical pipe to tap into when planning the location of a bathroom.

If there are recessed lighting fixtures in the ceilings of rooms below the attic, inspect the fixtures. Look at the electrical wiring to see that it is not damaged or spliced. Find any electrical outlets or fixtures.

You may decide to upgrade the insulation and use the attic strictly as storage or create a new living space. Whatever direction you go, you will need a building permit, so get advice from a contractor and the local building department during the early stages of your plan.

ATTIC WORKSHEET		
	NOTES	Image Recorder Reference
Stairs		
Width of steps		
Headroom in stairway		
Open or enclosed		
Location in house		
Adjoining walls		
Location in attic		
Headroom		
At the roof peak or highest dimension		
At the lowest sidewall		
Floor Plan of Living Space		
Length and width of floor space		
Length and width of floor space with 5 ft headroom		
Dimensions of Floor Joists		
Length and width		
Insulation		
Type and R-value (if any) in ceiling		
Type and R-value or depth (if any) in floor		

ATTIC WORKSHEET		Page 2
	NOTES	Image Recorder Reference
Recessed canlight fixtures		
Location of Permanent Fixtures		
Chimney		
Electrical wires		
Plumbing lines		
Heating ducts		
Built-ins		
Flooring		
Open, no finished floor		
Plywood sheathing or planks		
Attic Ceiling or Sheathing		
Rafters		
Sagging areas		
Signs of pest infestation or rot		
Moisture or condensation		
Fungus		
Vents		
Other issues		

Sketch attic floor plan:

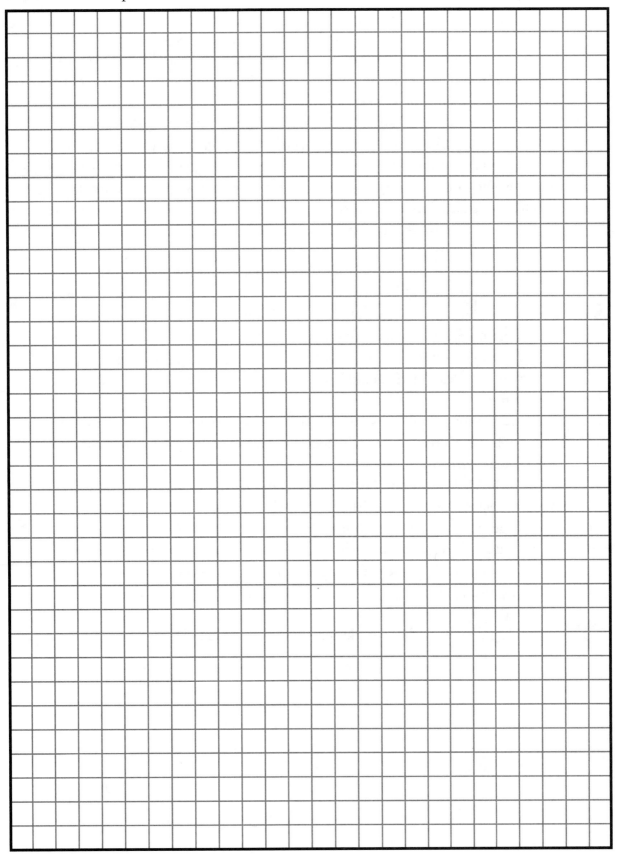

Porch Worksheet Instructions

While converting an open porch might offer expansion possibilities for interior space, consider the aesthetics of how it will impact the architecture on the exterior. When the conversion enhances the style and appearance of the house, it's an improvement worth making.

Use the "Porch Worksheet" to walk you through the process to consider the possibilities. Fill in the form to record the condition of the space, use a measuring tape to document dimensions, and make a sketch to give you an overview and note how it's attached to the house. Add a flashlight and knee pads to your gear to go underneath the porch to make a dimensioned sketch of the length and width of the four sides and the height of the walls to see how high it is off the ground.

Look at the size and direction of the floor joists and the spans of the main beams that bear the full load of the floor joists. Code specifications will vary according to the size of the porch, but 2- by 6-inch floor joists on 16-inch centers should be considered minimum.

Inspect the footings and posts in the corners and along the sides that support the porch. Brick piers should have all mortar joints filled and show no signs of cracking.

In the framing, look for signs of wood rot or damage from termites, carpenter ants, or beetles, any of which could require more extensive repair and replacement work.

Find the electrical lines, heating ducts, and plumbing pipes and note how they are routed under or near the porch. Also inspect the basement or crawl space adjacent to the porch and note the location of these utilities.

As you go through the worksheet, remember that converting a porch usually involves insulating the walls and ceiling, adding or upgrading windows, adding heat and electricity, and finishing the interior with wallboard, flooring, and woodwork.

You can download these worksheets from the included CD-Rom.

PORCH WORKSHEET		
	NOTES	Image Recorder Reference
Access to porch		
Adjoining what room		
Width of door/opening		
Floor plan of interior space		
Length, width, and height		
Walls and ceiling		
Cladding		
Condition		
Insulation		
Windows		
Sizes to remove		
Sizes to replace		
Flooring		
Material		
Condition		
Utilities		
Electrical receptacles		
Light fixtures		
Heating/cooling		
Foundation		
Length, width, and depth		
Material		
Condition		
Floor joists and beams		
Size and material		
Condition		
Covered with insulation		
Footings		
Location and number		
Condition		
Utilities		
Electrical lines		
Heating ducts		
Plumbing pipes		
Ground		
Condition of soil		
Other Issues		

Sketch porch floor plan:

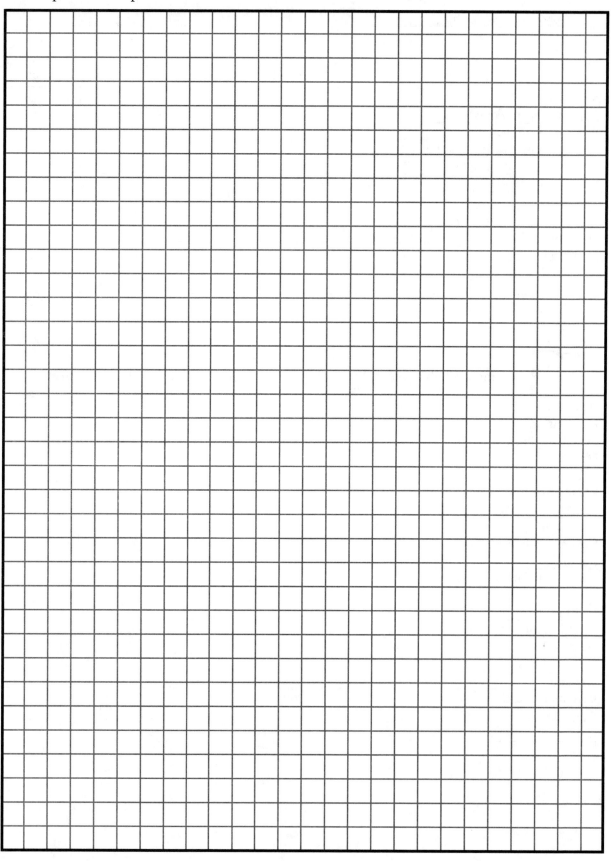

CHAPTER 7

MANAGING THE JOB

The word *multitasking* best describes the skill set required for managing a rehab project. Since the duration of work and what it costs are the keys to a quick turnaround, the ability to make things happen on time and on budget are the keys to a successful project. Planning the work schedule of a rehab property requires a different set of management skills from those needed in an office job. They include the ability to make on-the-spot decisions, schedule the work of subcontractors who have many other clients besides you, order the correct amounts of materials, cope with work delays and interruptions because of weather, and deal with building inspectors.

 To help with this long list of skills, use the worksheets and checklists in this chapter. You can download them from the included CD-Rom.

The following two checklists help you to evaluate a contractor and determine if the contract offered is a good one.

EVALUATING A CONTRACTOR CHECKLIST

☐ Does the contractor maintain a permanent mailing address, e-mail address, published personal phone number, fax number, and a cell phone, pager, or voice-messaging system? You want someone who can be reached easily.

☐ For how many years has the remodeling company been in business in the community? The longer the better because it suggests that the company is financially sound.

☐ Does the company have a relationship with qualified independent trade contractors such as plumbers and electricians who can be counted on? This is important to keep a project on track.

☐ Does the contractor have several customers for whom he or she completed projects similar to the one you're planning? You don't want to hire a pro skilled in framing new construction to remodel your small bathroom. A better choice is someone who specializes in the particular project you're planning.

☐ Will the contractor give you a list of customers you can call to ask if they are satisfied customers and if they'd hire the contractor again? Make the time to follow up and call the references.

☐ Is the contractor familiar with the types and ages of homes in your area? A contractor with such experience is more likely to know what he'll find behind the walls and under a floor than someone unfamiliar with the area.

☐ Who arranges for the building permit? The person who obtains the permit is the contractor of record and is liable for the work.

☐ Does the remodeling company offer a warranty? If so, what kind and for how long, and what's covered and what's not?

☐ Does the contractor agree to begin and complete your job within a reasonable timetable? And what's the fallout if there are delays?

☐ Will the contractor give you a list of his or her materials suppliers who extend him credit? Call them to see if the contractor has a good reputation for paying his or her bills.

☐ Does the contractor carry insurance that protects you from claims arising from property damage or job site injuries? Ask for a copy of the company's insurance certificate so that you can confirm that you won't be liable. Ask how much the project will add to the value of your home, and get additional insurance.

CHECKLIST FOR A GOOD CONTRACT

Look for these details and features in a remodeling project contract:

- ☐ Contractor's name, address, telephone, cell, and pager numbers and license information.

- ☐ Homeowner's name, address, home and business telephone and cell numbers, and location of the job site.

- ☐ Detailed job description of work to be completed, including protecting the surrounding area and daily and final cleanup work.

- ☐ Detailed list of all materials used in the project, including specifications of brand name and model number of all products, size, color, style, and any other descriptive information.

- ☐ Copies of and reference to drawings and specifications.

- ☐ Starting and completion dates and work hours and days that workers can be expected on the job.

- ☐ Specification that all the work performed will meet or exceed the building code.

- ☐ Specification of who will obtain any required building permits.

- ☐ Clearly spelled out financial terms, including the total price, payment schedule, and any cancellation penalty or early-completion incentive.

- ☐ Stipulation that the homeowner's signature is required for approval before work begins.

- ☐ Right of recession, which spells out that a homeowner can cancel a contract within three days of signing it.

- ☐ Procedure for change orders while the project is underway.

- ☐ Binding arbitration clause that lets both parties resolve a dispute quickly and effectively without expensive legal procedures.

- ☐ Warranty covering materials and workmanship for a minimum of a year.

- ☐ Assurance that the homeowner will not be liable for any third-party claims for nonpayment of materials or subcontractors.

Managing a House Rehab Checklist Instructions

A property owner is ultimately responsible for a major rehab project whether he or she is doing the project entirely himself or herself, acting as a general contractor, or has hired a contractor. With this in mind, it's key to be proactive in managing the project in whatever capacity you assume. The key issues involved in managing a job are staying in touch with subcontractors, being on top of the project's progress, and keeping track of the records and costs. If you're doing all the work yourself, managing can be daunting, and multitasking skills are the key to success.

No matter who is doing the work, it's important to keep records of the products and materials you use, the estimates for work, and a list of contact information for the various players involved in the project. You'll amass a pile of product information and a number of material samples, so delegate a crate in your vehicle to keep them handy. A folder or briefcase can keep bid sheets and correspondence in one place. Log the contact numbers of suppliers, contractors, and anyone else you call frequently into your cell phone so that reaching them is easy. Duplicating the information on a laptop, personal digital assistant (PDA), or whatever electronic device you're use to will help you to keep track of communications.

The "Managing a House Rehab Checklist" is designed as an overview of a project to help you to define the work required and record when it's completed. Use it to jot down repair items, things to replace, reminders, and whatever other information is pertinent to the project.

MANAGING A HOUSE REHAB CHECKLIST		
WORK DESCRIPTION	**NOTES**	**COMPLETED**
Exterior siding		
Condition		
Other issues		
Foundation		
Support columns or piers		
Exterior plumbing		
Spigot(s)		
Water meter		
Electrical service		
Meter		
Wires and cables		
Crawl space		
Condition of support posts, bolts		
Other issues		
Deck or patio		
Condition of material, railings		
Other issues		

MANAGING A HOUSE REHAB CHECKLIST		Page 2
WORK DESCRIPTION	NOTES	COMPLETED
Roof and chimney		
Flashing		
Gutters, downspouts, diverters		
Other issues		
Sidewalks and driveway		
Condition of surface		
Grading, low spots		
Doors and storm doors		
Condition		
Lock		
Storm screen and glass panels		
Door threshold		
Other issues		
Windows and storms		
Condition		
Glass		
Caulking		
Storm, screen, and glass panels		
Other issues		

MANAGING A HOUSE REHAB CHECKLIST		Page 3
WORK DESCRIPTION	NOTES	COMPLETED
Heating/cooling unit		
Condition		
Other issues		
Garage, outbuildings		
Siding		
Foundation and grading		
Doors and windows		
Roof, gutters, downspouts		
Interior floor and walls		
Electrical power		
Other issues		
Landscaping and trees		
Lawn		
Garden beds		
Trees and shrubbery		
Other issues		
Living/dining room		
Walls and ceiling		
Doors		
Windows		

MANAGING A HOUSE REHAB CHECKLIST

WORK DESCRIPTION	NOTES	COMPLETED
Floor		
Fireplace		
Built-ins		
Electric outlets		
Lighting		
HVAC		
Other issues		
Kitchen		
Walls and ceiling		
Doors		
Windows		
Floor		
Appliances: stove, oven, range, vent, refrigerator, disposal, dishwasher		
Sink and faucet		
Cabinets and countertops		
Electrical system		
GFCI outlets: adequate number and placement		
Lighting		
HVAC		
Other issues		

✔ MANAGING A HOUSE REHAB CHECKLIST		Page 5
WORK DESCRIPTION	NOTES	COMPLETED
Bathroom 1		
Walls and ceiling		
Doors		
Windows		
Floor		
Toilet		
Sink, faucet, cabinet		
Storage		
Accessories		
GFCI outlets: adequate number and placement okay		
Lighting		
HVAC		
Other issues		
Bathroom 2		
Walls and ceiling		
Doors		
Windows		
Floor		
Toilet		

MANAGING A HOUSE REHAB CHECKLIST		Page 6
WORK DESCRIPTION	NOTES	COMPLETED
Accessories		
Sink, faucet, cabinet		
Storage		
GFCI outlets: number and placement		
Lighting		
HVAC		
Other issues		
Bedroom 1		
Walls and ceiling		
Doors		
Windows		
Floor		
Closet		
Electrical		
Lighting		
HVAC		
Other issues		
Bedroom 2		
Walls and ceiling		
Doors		

	Page 7
MANAGING A HOUSE REHAB CHECKLIST	

WORK DESCRIPTION	NOTES	COMPLETED
Windows		
Floor		
Closet		
Electrical		
Lighting		
HVAC		
Other issues		
Bedroom 3		
Walls and ceiling		
Doors		
Windows		
Floor		
Closet		
Electrical		
Lighting		
HVAC		
Other issues		
Family Room		
Walls and ceiling		
Doors		
Windows		

MANAGING A HOUSE REHAB CHECKLIST		Page 8
WORK DESCRIPTION	NOTES	COMPLETED
Floor		
Fireplace		
Built-ins		
Electrical		
Lighting		
HVAC		
Other issues		
Halls and Closets		
Walls and ceiling		
Doors		
Windows		
Floor		
Stairs		
Smoke/CO detectors		
Other issues		
Attic		
Finished, unfinished		
Rafters		
Ventilation		
Insulation		

		Page 9
MANAGING A HOUSE REHAB CHECKLIST		
WORK DESCRIPTION	NOTES	COMPLETED
Stairs and access		
Other issues		
Basement		
Unfinished		
Partially finished		
Humidity, odors		
Water seepage		
Walls and ceiling		
Doors		
Windows		
Floor		
Lighting and electrical		
Plumbing pipes, water meter		
Stairs: balusters on steps, handrail on wall		
Laundry and Appliances		
Washer: braided stainless steel pressurized washer hoses, grounded		
Dryer: secure hose connection, vent to outside, grounded		
Other issues		

MANAGING A HOUSE REHAB CHECKLIST		Page 10
WORK DESCRIPTION	NOTES	COMPLETED
HVAC		
Furnace or heat pump		
Secure ductwork, clean filter		
Other issues		
Hot Water Heater		
Gas or electric, adequate capacity		
Other issues		
Electrical Service Panel		
Panel location		
Amperage voltage rating		
Number of circuits		
Limited or expandable		
Sump Pump and Floor Drain		
Location		
Type, size		
In working order		
Additional Notes		

Cost Estimates versus Actual and Change Order Worksheet Instructions

Before you begin any renovation of the property you should have a good idea as to its cost. In Chapter 5 we give you methods for estimating these costs, but however accurate the estimates are they are still estimates. Use the "Cost Estimates" sheet as a form that allows you to keep track of how your estimates compare to the actual bids submitted by the contractors. After the bids are in you can use this form to track the actual cost of the job compared to the contractor's bid. The form is very detailed so you may want to group all the items together if a contractor bid does not provide as detailed a breakout. If you are doing the work yourself compare your estimate to the actual cost of the work, in this case the materials.

Any deviation from the original estimate or the contractor's initial bid will increase the project's cost. It's very tempting to think to yourself or say to the contractor, "as long as you are taking that wall out let's add a few more windows." You can quickly lose control of the project's cost with just a few add-ons like this. Whenever a change in the original plan is contemplated, use the "Change Order" form to document the change and its associated cost. Make sure this cost is then added back into the original cost figures or else you won't be able to keep track of whether you are staying on budget. A few changes can easily be forgotten and add thousands of dollars to a project. Using change orders will prevent this or at least allow you to keep track of these additional costs.

COST ESTIMATES VS ACTUAL			
	Estimate	**Bid**	**Actual**
Permits, fees	_____	_____	_____
Utilities	_____	_____	_____
Excavation	_____	_____	_____
Foundation	_____	_____	_____
Rough lumber	_____	_____	_____
Rough labor	_____	_____	_____
Doors	_____	_____	_____
Windows	_____	_____	_____
Roofing	_____	_____	_____
Concrete flatwork	_____	_____	_____
Siding	_____	_____	_____
Plumbing	_____	_____	_____
Heating	_____	_____	_____
Electrical	_____	_____	_____
Insulation	_____	_____	_____
Water (well)	_____	_____	_____
Sewer (septic)	_____	_____	_____
Fireplaces	_____	_____	_____
Drywall	_____	_____	_____
Cabinets	_____	_____	_____
Interior trim	_____	_____	_____
Trim labor	_____	_____	_____
Painting	_____	_____	_____
Appliances	_____	_____	_____
Light fixtures	_____	_____	_____
Floor coverings	_____	_____	_____
Driveway	_____	_____	_____
Garage door	_____	_____	_____
Other	_____	_____	_____
Subtotal	_____	_____	_____
Misc.	_____	_____	_____
Total	_____	_____	_____

CHANGE ORDER

Date: _____

Original date of contract: _____

Property address: _____

Property owner: _____

Contractor: _____

Change order number: _____

Request for Change Order

The undersigned owner and contractor agree to approve and perform work that is substantially different from the original scope of the project. Both parties know that the requested changes, which are listed below, may change the price and completion schedule. Any differences in the cost of the project relating to this change order will be taken into account for the regular payment schedule.

The contractor will perform the following work:

_____

_____

_____

_____

_____

_____

_____

The total cost for labor and materials to be added or deducted:

How the change will affect the completion schedule:

New estimated completion date:

Contractor approval and date:

Signature: _____

Owner approval and date:

Signature: _____

Punch List Instructions

A *punch list* is a contractor's to-do list of everything that is not completed or anything that requires fixing or replacement. As a property owner, you should keep a close eye on the progress of work and keep your own punch list of things needing repair or correction. Use the following "Punch List" so that when you communicate regularly with the contractor, you can point out the items and look for others.

PUNCH LIST

Property owner: _____

Property address: _____

Contact information: _____

General or subcontractor: _____

Contact information: _____

Punch List Items	Date	Approved by
_____	_____	
_____	_____	
_____	_____	
_____	_____	
_____	_____	
_____	_____	
_____	_____	
_____	_____	
_____	_____	
_____	_____	
_____	_____	

Completed punch list items submitted by: _____

Contractor: _____

All items accepted as completed by: _____

Owner: _____

CHAPTER 8

RENTING AS A FALLBACK STRATEGY

Being a landlord can be one path to a successful real estate strategy, especially when you invest long term and can wait to sell the property when prices are at their peak. In a slow market, a rental property can hold its own while you wait for prices to rise, and tenants pay the monthly cost of keeping the property as part of your investment portfolio.

The worksheets and calculators in this chapter give you a detailed look at the numbers and allow you to analyze a property's potential as a rental. The checklists are guidelines to managing and maintaining rental property and keeping it appreciating in value.

You can download these worksheets and checklists from the included CD-Rom.

Finding a Good Tenant

One of the most important elements in having a successful rental strategy is finding a reliable tenant. These first three forms provide you with some tools to gather information about the prospective tenant. Then once you have found a suitable candidate the other two checklists will help you establish a good relationship with the tenant.

The Tenant Application is probably the most important document and should be completed very carefully. The discrimination laws require you to have a factual reason to turn down an applicant, such as a poor credit history or less than glowing references. This form if properly filled out will be the documentation of your selection procedures.

Follow up on all the topics and take notes or attach documents like credit reports and comments made during your discussions with employers and former landlords. Save these documents even after you have selected a tenant. The forms will provide you with a second choice if the first tenant does not work out. This documentation will also become essential evidence should you face a discrimination lawsuit.

The landlord checklist is a tool that you can use to make sure the rental unit is ready for the tenant to occupy. It will also be your record that everything was in working order and checked out before the tenant moves in. After the tenant occupies the unit, follow up, and check that they actually contacted the utilities and established accounts.

The Landlord Walk-through form allows you to document the condition of the property before the tenant takes possession, during their stay and before they leave. It's important that you inspect the property on a regular schedule. At the time the lease is renewed or before the tenant moves out, a walk-through is a must. This will give you and your tenant a time to discuss the condition of the property. Normal wear and tear is expected but unless you periodically inspect the property you have no way of assessing its condition. This is also a great tool to use when discussing improvements or updates the tenant may want. Edit the contents of each topic to match your property profile.

Tenant Application

Tenant name: _____

Employer name: _____

Monthly income: _____

_____

Credit and bank information:

   Checking: _____

_____

_____

_____

   Savings:

_____

_____

_____

   Credit cards: _____

_____

_____

   Credit report authorization:

_____

Auto information:

   Driver's license number:

_____

   License plate number:

_____

Rental history (list three):

1. _____

_____

2. _____

_____

3. _____

_____

_____

Personal references (list three):

1. _____

_____

2. _____

_____

3. _____

_____

LANDLORD PREOCCUPANCY CHECKLIST

After screening and selecting a tenant, use this checklist before the tenant takes occupancy.

☐ Verify your landlord insurance, and make sure that you know what is covered and what is not. Explain this to the tenant.

☐ Verify if tenant or lawn service is responsible for cutting the lawn.

☐ Make plans to clean gutters in the Spring and Fall.

☐ Add a routine drive-by to your monthly calendar to check condition of the property.

☐ Test all gas and electrical appliances to make sure that they operate correctly and safely.

☐ Test all lights, faucets, sinks, and other devices to ensure that they operate correctly and safely.

☐ Install fresh batteries in smoke and CO detectors.

☐ Install a clean filter in the furnace and have a replacement supply available for the tenants to use.

☐ Label fuses in electrical circuit panel box for the rooms they service.

☐ Contact the utility providers to arrange meter readings and advise tenants about how to have the accounts put in their name.

☐ Provide duplicate keys for all locks.

☐ Walk through the property with a digital camera and document all rooms, the exterior, and the yard as a dated record of their condition.

☐ Provide operating instructions for all appliances.

☐ Provide written instructions on how to contact you.

Landlord Postoccupancy Walk-through

Before a tenant vacates rental property, it's a good idea for the landlord to walk through and inspect its condition. Use this list to examine all the features of the property and make sure that everything is in the same good condition as when the tenant moved in.

Front Entry—overall condition
Are the door and lock in working order? Did the tenant return the key? Check the storm door to see that there's no broken glass or torn screen. Is the mailbox firmly attached?

Living, Dining, Family Rooms—overall condition
Inspect all rooms from the ceiling down to the walls and then the floor. Is it clean and are all furnishings removed? Look for holes in the wall and signs of wear on the wall behind the doors where the knob often creates a dent. Does the paint or wallcovering need to be replaced? Is the woodwork clean and finished? Is the flooring or carpeting in good condition? Does it need to be cleaned or replaced? What's the condition of a fireplace or built-in cabinets? Do the doors close and door locks operate? Do windows open and close, and are there any broken glass panes or torn screens?

Check the light fixtures to see that they work. Also use a small electric appliance such as a hair dryer to confirm that all the electric outlets are in good working order.

Kitchen—overall condition
Are the walls and ceiling clean and free of a buildup of grease, especially behind the range. Does the paint or wallcovering need to be replaced? Is the woodwork clean and finished? Is the flooring material clean and in good condition? Open the cabinets to see that the hinges operate, and make sure that everything is removed from them. Check out the countertop and fixtures to see that they're in good condition and in working order.

Inspect all the appliances, and turn them on to confirm that they are empty, clean, and in good working order.

Bathroom—overall condition
Are the walls and ceilings, especially around the bathtub/shower, clean and in good condition? Does the paint or wallcovering need to be replaced? Inspect the condition of the tub/shower surround to see that there's no water damage. Look at the vanity cabinet and countertop for signs of wear. Is the bathroom a safe environment with grab bars and nonslippery surfaces? Is the flooring material a nonskid surface? Look for gaps around countertops and the tub for leaks and damaged caulk that needs to be replaced.

Operate the fixtures. Turn on the faucets and flush the toilet to make sure that all things work. Test the door and window for operation, too.

Bedrooms—overall condition
Inspect the rooms from the ceiling down to the walls and then the floor. Is the room clean, and are all furnishings removed? Look for holes in the wall and signs of wear on the wall behind the doors where the knob often creates a dent. Does the paint or wallcovering need to be replaced? Is the woodwork clean and finished? Is the flooring or carpeting in good condition? Does it need to be cleaned or replaced? Do the doors close and door locks operate? Do windows open and close, and are there any broken glass panes or torn screens? Are closets empty complete with a clothes rod and shelving?

Check the light fixtures to see that they work. Also use a small electric appliance such as a hair dryer to confirm all the electric outlets are in good working order.

Attic, Basement—overall condition
If it's a storage area, is it clean, dry, and empty of all contents? If it's finished, is the space clean, free of debris, and ready for occupancy?

Systems
Has any damage been done to the heating and cooling systems, their thermostats, or the hot-water heater?

Back Entry, Garage—overall condition
Is the back or side entrance door and lock in working order? Did the tenant return the keys? Check the storm door to see that there's no broken glass or torn screen. Does the garage door operate, and did you find the remote control unit in working order? Is the garage clean of belongings and debris? If you supplied garbage cans, are they accounted for?

Lawn and Garden—overall condition
Is the lawn cut, and are garden beds maintained in the condition they were when the tenants moved in? Did the tenants remove all their outdoor furniture and equipment from the yard?

NOTES

_____

_____

_____

Using the Maintenance Reminder Checklists

By its very nature, a house and all its systems need routine maintenance to keep them working. Inside a house, the heating and cooling systems require periodic tuneups to keep them operating at peak performance. Any place there's water or moisture requires watching so that it doesn't damage surrounding surfaces. And the ongoing growth of trees and shrubs, not to mention the lawn, needs a continual routine of trimming and pruning.

Whether you live in the property or rent it to tenants, a house continues to get dirty, be affected by the elements, and have its systems wear down. Use the "Home Maintenance Reminder Checklist" as a guideline to managing the maintenance of your property. You'll see that it is compiled in two formats. Use whichever format you find the most useful, and keep your property in tip-top shape.

If you rent the property with the arrangement that the tenant will treat the home as if it is his or her own, including performing the maintenance chores, give the tenant a copy of the "Home Maintenance Reminder Checklist." The checklist doesn't include weekly chores such as maintaining a clean house or on-demand jobs such as lawn care or snow removal, so be sure to clarify who is responsible for doing those jobs.

HOME MAINTENANCE REMINDER CHECKLIST			
Inspections/Routines	Monthly	6 Months	Yearly
Change furnace and heat pump filters as needed	X		
Clean/change filter in window air conditioners when in use	X		
Furnace tune-up			X
Heat pump tune-up			X
Replace batteries in smoke and CO detectors		X	
Check that fire extinguishers are fully charged	X		
Inspect caulking around tubs and sinks and replace as needed		X	
Wash windows		X	
Remove sediment from buildup in hot-water tank heater			X
Inspect attic for signs of roof leaks			X
Lubricate, test, and clean sump pump		X	
Inspect siding, foundation, and roof for damage		X	
Hire a chimney sweep to inspect and clean chimney			X
Inspect exterior heat pump or air-conditioning units and clear debris			X
Clear outdoor clothes dryer vent of lint buildup		X	
Power wash deck and siding			X

Clear gutters/downspouts for runoff, and check for leaks		X	
Inspect exterior siding for signs of termite or wood damage		X	
Inspect exterior caulking and weatherstripping around doors and windows		X	
Inspect and tune up garage door opener mechanism and gasket			X
Inspect and clean sliding door track			X
Examine drainage field of septic system			X
Wash storm door frame, panel, and windows		X	
Plug air leaks in siding or foundation with spray-foam insulation			X
Prune trees, shrubs, and vines		X	

HOME MAINTENANCE REMINDER CHECKLIST

Monthly

Change furnace and heat pump filters as needed

Clean/change filter in window air conditioners when in use

Check that fire extinguishers are fully charged

Every 6 Months

Replace batteries in smoke and CO detectors

Inspect caulking around tubs and sinks and replace as needed

Wash windows

Lubricate, test, and clean sump pump

Inspect siding, foundation, and roof for damage

Clean outdoor clothes dryer vent of lint buildup

Clear gutters/downspouts for runoff, and check for leaks

Inspect exterior siding for signs of termites or wood damage

Inspect exterior caulking and weatherstripping around doors and windows

Wash storm door frame, panel, and windows

Prune trees, shrubs and vines

Yearly

Tune up furnace or heat pump

Remove sediment buildup from hot water heater

Inspect attic for signs of roof leaks

Hire a chimney sweep to inspect and clean chimney

Inspect exterior heat pump or air-conditioning unit and clear debris

Power wash deck and siding

Inspect and tune up garage door opener mechanism and gasket

Inspect and clean sliding door track

Examine drainage field of septic system

Plug air leaks in siding or foundation with spray-foam insulation

Rental Property Loan Calculator

In Chapter 1 you'll find a loan calculator tool that shows you the monthly payment on a loan given the interest rate, loan amount, and its term in years. This type of calculator is useful because the lending institution bases the size of the loan on the value of the property and your personal ability to repay it. Once you learn the loan amount and terms, you can calculate the monthly payments for interest and principal.

When you talk to a lending institution about financing rental property, the lending institution does not consider the value of the property as important as its income potential because this will be the main source for the funds to repay the loan. The calculator that follows analyzes the cash flow of a rental property. After you enter the data, it will tell you the size of a loan a lender probably will be willing to make.

The major variables, such as rent, mortgage rate, terms, and occupancy rate, are at the top of the calculator. Most lenders like to keep at least a 1.2 debt-repayment ratio. This gives them a little cushion and keeps the loan payments lower than the property income. This calculator assumes this debt-repayment ratio; if your institution has different requirements, then change the ratio.

The other variables are self-explanatory and come from your financial records. In this case, the utilities are paid by the tenant, and that line is left empty, and there are not condo fees. This calculator does not take into consideration the value of the property. But you can use it to estimate the amount of equity you would be able to withdraw should you refinance. For example, let's say that your present loan is paid down to $55,000; then, with the property's current cash flow, the lender would be willing to lend up to $111,478. If you refinance and pay off your present loan, you would have $56,478 to put into improvements or for other uses.

If you don't download this calculator, then type the formulas in the following table into the indicated spreadsheet cells of a blank Excel spreadsheet. Note that the cells F7 to F10 and F15 to F20 are variables and are referenced by other cells. Cell F14 contains a formula to calculate the lost rental income. Cell F25 contains the variable for the debt ratio. A ratio of 1.2 income to debt is a standard requirement for most banks.

Most of the calculation is done in the H column. H12 sums up the monthly rent and cells H22 to H27 contain the formulas that do most of the work. The maximum monthly loan payment the bank will allow is in H26. Cell H27 uses the present value (PV) function. The value of the loan interest is in cell F8 and is divided by 12 because the loan period is in years. The loan term is in cell F9 and is multiplied by 12 because it is in years and a negative sign is inserted

A	B	C	D	E	F	G	H	I
3								
4		Rental Property Loan Calculator						
5								
6								
7		Rent (Monthly)			$1,200.00			
8		Mortgage Rate (%)			7.0%			
9		Mortgage Time (Years)			30			
10		Rental Occupancy (%)			95%			
11								
12		Annual Rent					$14,400.00	
13		Operating Expenses						
14		Lost Rent			$720.00			
15		Taxes			$1,200.00			
16		Insurance			$1,000.00			
17		Utilities						
18		Repairs/Maintenance			$600.00			
19		Condo Fees						
20		Advertising			$200.00			
21		Other						
22		Total Expense					$3,720.00	
23		Yearly Net Cash Flow					$10,680.00	
24		Monthly Cash Flow					$890.00	
25		Debt Repayment Ratio			1.2			
26		Monthly Debt Load					$741.67	
27		Approx. Size of Loan					$111,478.11	
28								

before the monthly loan payment H26 because these are outward cash flows, since you are paying the loan.

Enter the formulas in the cells and then check your spreadsheet by entering the same numbers in the Rental Property Loan Calculator. If the spreadsheet is accurate the answers should be the same. If not go back and check that the formulas are correct and entered in the correct cells.

F14=H12-(H12*F10)

H12=F7*12

H22=SUM(F14:F20)

H23=H12-H22

H24=H23/12

H26=IF(F25,H24/F25,0)

H27=PV(F8/12,F9*12,-H26,0,0)

Rental Property Analysis Worksheet

The "Rental Property Analysis Worksheet" analyzes a rental property cash flow and calculates the rate of return. The spreadsheet is easy to use because the variables are at the top of the sheet. As you fill in these variables, the spreadsheet calculates the mortgage payments and cash flow. You can change any of the variables, such as the rent and occupancy rate, to see how these changes affect the bottom line. The yearly appreciation and holding period can be changed to see how different market conditions affect the property's profitability.

For example, if you sold the property without an agent, you would enter zero under "Sales Agent Rate" and save $9,500, which goes right to the bottom line. Remember that as the holding period gets longer, there's a higher chance that many of these variables will change; the spreadsheet does not take this into consideration.

If you don't download this calculator, then type the formulas in the table below into the indicated spreadsheet cells in a new Excel spreadsheet. This spreadsheet is large, so it's important to keep track of the columns and rows as you enter the formulas.

All the text labels are in columns C and G. Cells at the top of the spreadsheet are variables and their values are used in the spreadsheet formulas; only cells E8 and E9 contain formulas to calculate the down payment and loan amount. Cell E20 calculates the yearly rent and E21 calculates the loss of revenue due to nonoccupancy. Cells E24 and H24 use the payment function (PMT) to calculate the mortgage payment. Cells E35 and H35 use the future value (FV) function to calculate the increase in value of the property over time.

	A	B	C	D	E	F	G	H	I
1									
2									
3					Rental Property Analysis Worksheet				
4									
5									
6			Cost		$159,000.00		Rent		$1,200.00
7			Downpayment %		10%		Occupancy Rate %		95%
8			Downpayment amount		$15,900.00		Management Fee %		0%
9			Loan		$143,100.00		Sales Agent Rate %		5%
10			Mgt. Rate		7.0%		Yearly Appreciation %		3%
11			Mgt. Time		30		Holding Period (years)		5
12			Insurance, Taxes		$1,400.00				
13			Condo Fee		$1,900.00				
14			Improvements		$5,000.00				
15			Misc.		$500.00				
16									
17									
18					*One Year*			*Over Time*	
19			**Income**						
20			Rent		$14,400.00			$72,000.00	
21			Occupancy Reduction		$720.00			$3,600.00	
22			Anticipated Rent			$13,680.00			$68,400.00
23			**Expenses**						
24			Mgt. Payment		$11,531.91			$57,659.57	
25			Insurance, Taxes		$1,400.00			$7,000.00	
26			Management Fees						
27			Misc.		$500.00			$2,500.00	
28			Condo Fees		$1,900.00			$9,500.00	
29			Total Expenses			$15,331.91			$76,659.57
30			Cash Flow			$(1,651.91)			$(8,259.57)
31									
32			**Anticipated Appreciation**						
33									
34			Cost		$159,000.00			$159,000.00	
35			Increase		$4,770.00			$25,324.58	
36			Future Value			$163,770.00			$184,324.58
37			Sales Cost		$8,188.50			$9,216.23	
38			Pay Mgt.		$143,100.00			$143,100.00	
39			Cash Payments			$151,288.50			$152,316.23
40			Net Cash			$12,481.50			$32,008.35
41			Investment + Improvements			$20,900.00			$20,900.00
42			Gain from Sale			$(8,418.50)			$11,108.35
43			Cash Flow			$(1,651.91)			$(8,259.57)
44			Anticipated Profit			$(10,070.41)			$2,848.78
45			Return			−48%			14%
46									

E8=(E6*E7)
E9=E6-(E6*E7)
E20=(I6*12)
E21=E20-(E20*I7)
E24=IF(I10,(PMT(E10,E11,-E9,0,0)),0)

E25=E12
E26=E20*I8
E27=E157
E28=E13
E34=E6
E35=(E6*I10)
E37=F36*I9
E38=E9

H20=(I6*12)*I11

H21=(E20-(E20*I7))*I11

H24=IF(I10,((PMT(E10,E11,-E9,0,0))*I11),0)

H25=E12*I11

H26=H26

H27=E15*I11

H28=E13*I11

H34=E6

H35=((FV(I10,I11,0,E6,0))*-1)-E6

H37=I36*I9

H38=E9

F22=E20-E21
F29=SUM(E24:E28)
F30=F22-F29
F36=SUM(E34:E35)
F39=E37+E38

F40=F36-F39

F41=E8+E14

F42=F40-F41

F43=F30

F44=SUM(F42:F43)

F45=IF(F41,(F44/F41),0)

I22=H20-H21
I29=SUM(H24:H28)
I30=I22-I29
I36=SUM(H34:H35)
I39=H37+H38
I40=I36-I39
I41=E8+E14
I42=I40-I41
I43=I30
I44=I42+I43
I45=IF(I41,(I44/I41),0)

CROSSWORD
PUZZLES

Real Estate For Rookies

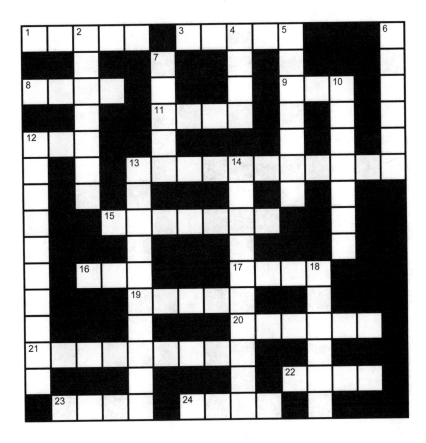

Across

1. Written agreement

3. Proposal to buy property

8. 180-by-242-feet of land

9. Adjustable rate mortgage (abbr.)

11. Like-new condition

12. Federal Housing Administration (abbr.)

13. Court action due to loan default

15. Way-below asking price offer

16. Offer to buy

17. Property sold in current condition

19. One percent loan fee

20. Funds set aside and held in trust

21. Determines value of real estate

22. Money owed to another

23. Legal claim against property

24. Hard surface covering walls and floors

Down

2. Being behind in payments

4. Apartment unit

5. Member of Nat'l Assn. of Realtors

6. Short-term loan

7. Loan exceeding $417,000

10. House built in sections in a factory

12. Federal Home Loan Mortgage Corp. (abbr.)

13. Area vulnerable to high water

14. Asset pledged as loan security

18. Drawing with precise legal boundaries

Parts of a House

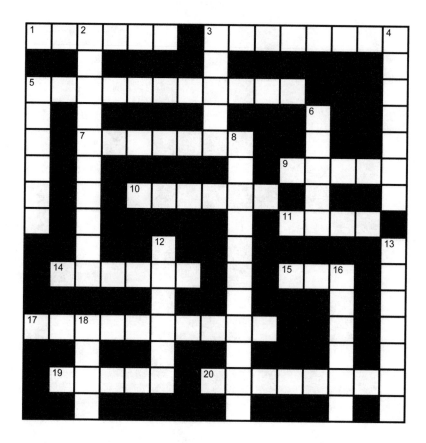

Across

1. Exterior of a building

3. Window hinged at side

5. Classic design

7. Platform between flights of stairs

9. Upper level of house

10. Window hinged at top and swings outward

11. Roof that slopes in one direction

14. Decorative molding

15. Roof with four sloping sides

17. Ornately carved wood

19. Vertical board between stair treads

20. Closely spaced support for a railing

Down

2. Area beneath a house

3. Decorative ceiling molding

4. Space between base cabinet and floor

5. Miniature tower

6. Slope of roof

8. Highly decorative woodwork

12. Column

13. French roof

16. Square base for a column

18. Horizontal trim work

Home-Buying Basics

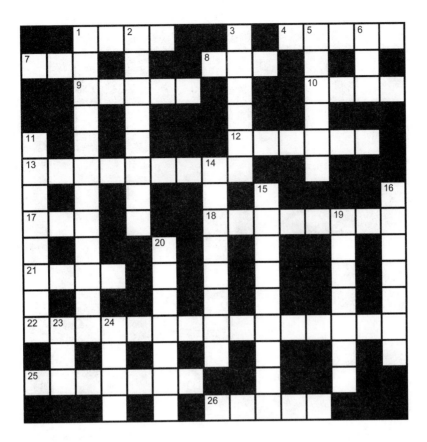

Across

1. Money owed to another

4. Time to clear or bounce a check for payment

7. Good faith estimate (abbr.)

8. Dept. of Housing and Urban Development (abbr.)

9. One percent of amount of a mortgage

10. Comparable property

12. Difference between value and debt

13. Professional who designs buildings

17. Federal Housing Administration (abbr.)

18. Changeable interest rate

21. Current condition, no warranties

22. Fixer-Upper

25. Payment made after it is due

26. Proposal to buy property

Down

1. Decline in property value

2. Permanently attached cabinets

3. Detail plan of income/expenses

5. Time period when lender guarantees interest rate

6. Adjustable-rate mortgage (abbr.)

11. Bathroom without shower or tub

14. Legally binding rule

15. In perfect, move-in condition

16. Failure to make payment

19. Wall that supports a roof or part of a building

20. Residence where someone lives most often

23. Annual percentage rate (abbr.)

24. Legal document that conveys title

Tooling Around

Across

5. Applies paint
6. Type of hammer
9. Saw that cuts plastic and metal
10. Heavy-duty stapler
12. Drives/removes hex nuts/bolts
14. Countersinks a nail
18. Snakelike device for clogs
19. Crank handle hand drill
20. Allen wrench
21. Crowbar-like tool
23. Finishes wet concrete
24. Tool used with a mallet

Down

1. Narrow metal bars
2. Plumber's friend
3. Flexible metal blade to remove paint
4. Hammer that drives small nails
7. Type of pliers
8. Blade screwdriver
11. Wrench with ratchet mechanism
13. Measuring tape
15. Applies adhesive
16. Heavy plumbing wrench
17. Flexible knife for patching
22. Ice pick-like tool

Bathroom Makeover

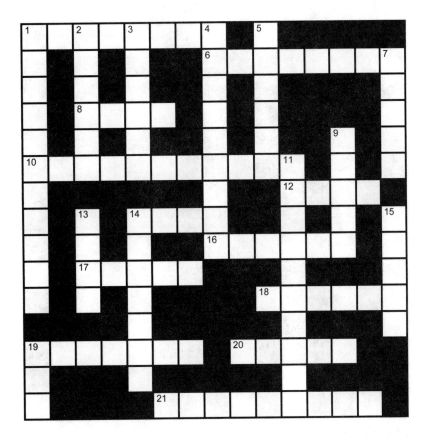

Across

1. Measuring tape

6. Bathtub in an alcove

8. Fungus growth in damp area

10. Toilet

12. Heating, ventilation, air conditioning (abbr.)

14. Ground fault circuit interrupter (abbr.)

16. Row of tiles

17. Colors wood

18. Sliding door in a wall

19. Wallboard

20. Water-based paint

21. Seals drywall joints

Down

1. Heats towels and room

2. Issued by building department

3. Paint application tool

4. Designed for ease and comfortable use

5. Decorative wall light

7. Someone who does it himself-or herself

9. Unclogs a drain

11. Device that measures temperature of a room

13. Lighting a particular area

14. Bathtub aid

15. Distributes warm or cool air through a house

19. Drain waste vent system (abbr.)

Remodeling

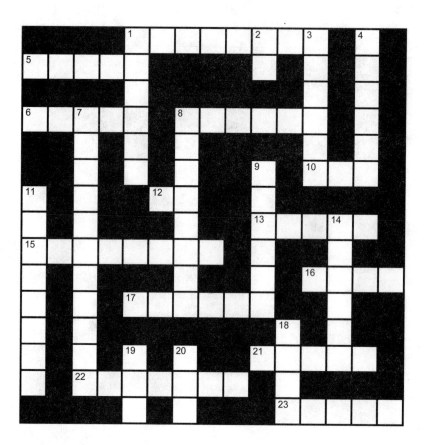

Across

1. Surface below a finished floor
5. Parallel horizontal framing
6. Short, round length of wood
8. Shelf above fireplace
10. Energy efficiency rating (abbr.)
12. Underwriters Laboratory (abbr.)
13. Two levels of adjacent surfaces
15. Floor of shower
16. Molding with a concave face
17. Forms seal between parts
21. Overhang of a roof
22. Window above a door
23. Shallow sink

Down

1. Vertical struts of a panel door
2. On center (abbr.)
3. Insulation resistance to heat flow
4. Seals surface
7. Toilet
8. Divides glass in a window
9. Underside of eaves
11. Wood from deciduous trees
14. Decorative wall light
18. Top and sides of door
19. Heavy wood screw bolt
20. Oriented-strand board (abbr.)

Selling Your House Savvy

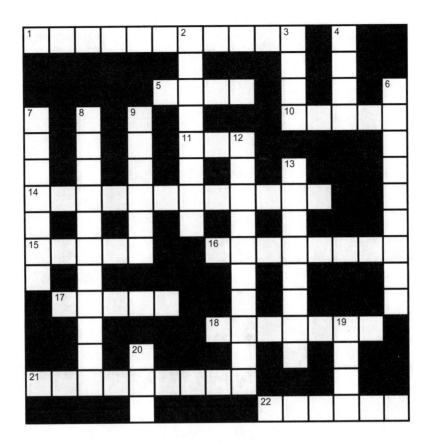

Across

1. Someone whose children have moved out

5. For Sale By Owner (abbr.)

10. Property ownership document

11. Multiple Listing Service (abbr.)

14. Local regulation about construction

15. Written agreement

16. Fee charged to borrow money

17. Acts on behalf of buyer or seller

18. House built in sections in factory

21. Federal National Mortgage Assn.(abbr.)

22. Buying a more expensive house

Down

2. Right given to use or access property

3. Monthly payment to occupy property

4. Just like new condition

6. Measure of ability to repay a loan

7. Way-below-market offer

8. Profit on an investment

9. In between loan

12. Vacation home

13. Addition to contract

19. 180-by-242 foot plot of land

20. Offer to buy

Lawn and Garden

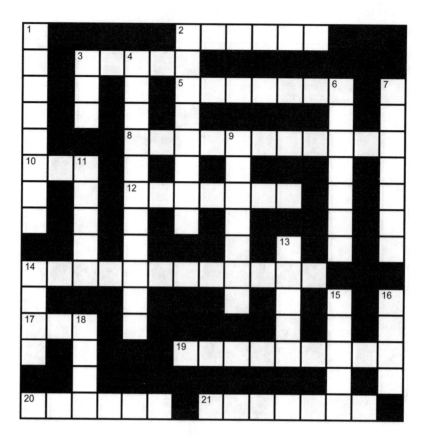

Across

2. Plant that grows in one season
3. Bushes planted close together
5. Condition caused by poor drainage
8. Taking up dead plant material
10. Integrated Pest Management (abbr.)
12. Wearing away of soil
14. Science of gardening
17. Fluid in plants
19. Heavy pavers
20. Borders a garden bed
21. Type of grass

Down

1. Removing overcrowded seedlings
2. Loosening soil to allow air passage
3. Long handled cultivating tool
4. Removing spent flowers
6. Shrub undergrowth
7. No chemical gardening
9. Alkalinity of soil
11. Push or power device that cuts lawn
13. Lawn
14. Distributes water
15. Limbs of a palm tree
16. Tall grass in shallow water
18. Well-rooted seedling in cellular tray

ANSWERS
FOR
CROSSWORD
PUZZLES

Real Estate for Rookies

Parts of a House

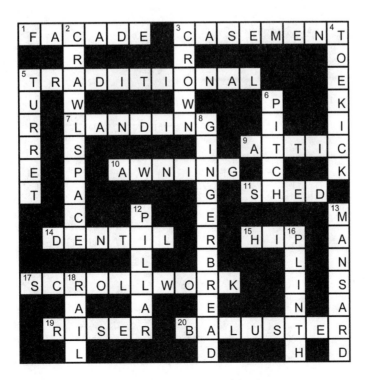

Home-Buying Basics

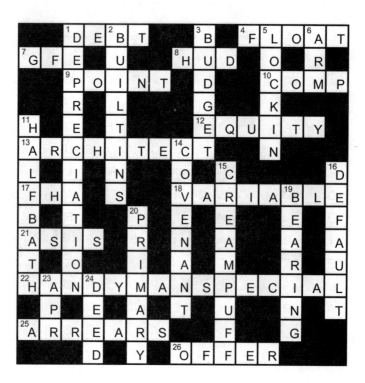

Tooling Around

Bathroom Makeover

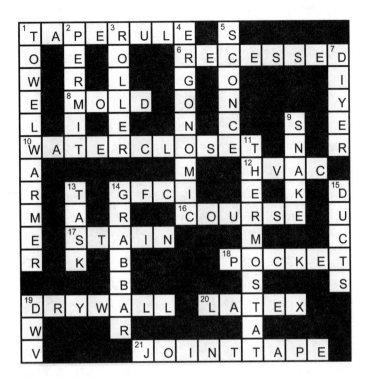

Remodeling

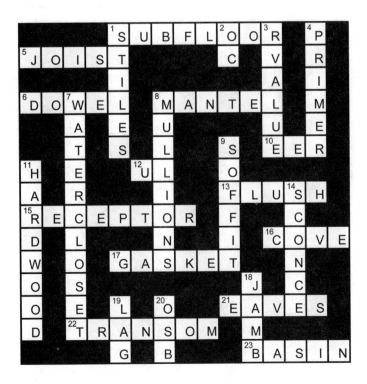

Selling Your House Savvy

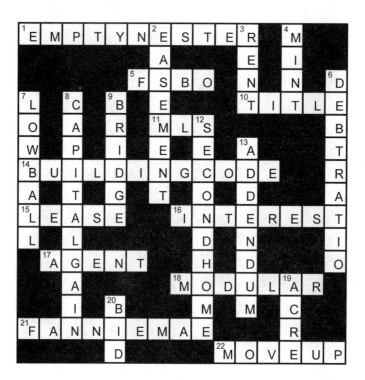

Lawn and Garden

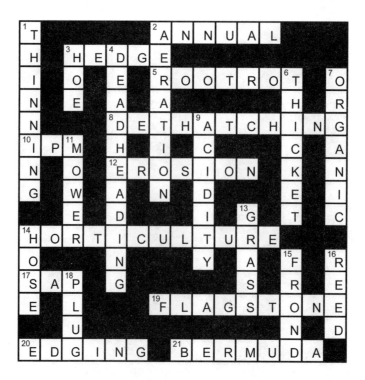

About the Authors

Katie and Gene Hamilton rehabbed their first home in 1966 and were soon buying and rehabbing houses full-time. The authors of several home improvement and real estate books, they also write the nationally syndicated newspaper column "Do It Yourself . . . Or Not?." They are founders of HouseNet.com, one of the first home improvement sites on the Internet and AOL. They have appeared on CNN, HGTV, *Today*, *Dateline*, and several other programs.